MIKE OAKLEY was born and brought up in Dorset before moving to Bristol in the mid 1960s where he had a career in town and country planning until retirement in 1996.

Mike's interest in the history and role of railway stations and halts in the evolving social and economic life of the West Country led to the preparation and publication of a successful series of books, all of which have been well received by local historians and railway enthusiasts.

Published by the Dovecote Press, the series was 'Discover Dorset' Railway Stations (2001), Somerset Railway Stations (2002), Gloucestershire Railway Stations (2003), Wiltshire Railway Stations (2004), Devon Railway Stations (2007) and Cornwall Railway Stations (2009).

Of particular interest is how stations have changed over the years, the new uses now in place where they have closed and also clues to the former railway use. Having originally visited them in early 2002, Mike has now revisited the 180 station and halt sites in Somerset. This book is the result of the new research, including many 'then and now' illustrations and a schedule that sets out the current situation at all sites.

SOMERSET STATIONS
Then and Now

MIKE OAKLEY

THE DOVECOTE PRESS

First published in 2011 by The Dovecote Press Ltd
Stanbridge, Wimborne Minster, Dorset BH21 4JD

ISBN 978-1-904-34994-5
Text © Mike Oakley 2011
Photographs © Mike Oakley 2011 (also see Acknowledgements)

Designed by The Dovecote Press
Printed and bound in Singapore by KHL

All papers used by The Dovecote Press are natural,
recyclable products made from wood grown in sustainable,
well-managed forests

A CIP catalogue record for this book is available
from the British Library

1 3 5 7 9 8 6 4 2

CONTENTS

INTRODUCTION

Over the last ten years the author has researched the history, development and role of the railway stations and halts in South West England. This research led to the publication between 2001 and 2009 of a series of books on these stations and halts, each one relating to the region's counties. They include a short history of the county's passenger rail network, an account of the history and role of each station and halt and one or more historic photographs of each one. During the research the author visited virtually every site, including those where all traces of the railway have now gone. Particular note was made of the current use of the railway buildings that survive, whether or not in railway use, and also the site where this was now in another use. Photographs of the current situation were taken but very few were included in the books.

One of the earliest books was that relating to Somerset. Site visits were made early in 2002 and the book (now out of print) was published that autumn. This current book seeks to up-date the position and significantly includes many photographs of the current use of the buildings and sites as viewed in 2010 and 2011, when repeat visits were undertaken. Alongside these new photographs are earlier historic photographs and also captions explaining the changes. In many cases the historic photographs of the stations/halts are different from those in the previous book. Also included is a schedule of all the 180 stations and halts that one time served the county of Somerset and details are given of the 2010/2011 situation. This new book is thus a complementary and companion volume to the 2002 work.

The South West has a rich railway history and its stations and halts exhibit a wide variety of styles and building materials reflecting, in many cases, designs adopted by the railway companies that built the line. Often a focal point for the town or village community, many were constructed of local materials, making the buildings, including ticket offices and waiting rooms, goods sheds, signal boxes and station master's houses, of considerable architectural merit. Unfortunately many of these buildings have been demolished and a few lie derelict, but others remain still in railway use or have been renovated for new uses such as houses, offices and warehouses. In other cases the former sites of the stations and associated goods yards have been redeveloped for new uses, in particular housing or industrial estates and supermarkets. These uses have come about as many of the former railway stations and yards now form valuable sites within expanded towns and villages.

The county of Somerset, at one time served by some 180 stations and halts, contains many good examples of these changing situations. Today only 19 stations remain open on the county's main railway network. In some cases the station building has changed very little since its opening (eg Bridgwater and Yatton). In others there are marked differences for instance, at Somerset's largest station, Taunton, where the current station dates mainly from the early 1930s, replacing the earlier station with an overall roof. Sadly in many cases the early attractive buildings have been demolished and replaced by modern metal and glass shelters on the surviving platforms (eg Bruton).

A happier situation prevails on the restored West Somerset Railway where the original station structures have been beautifully restored, creating an atmosphere that brings back the ambience of the early steam era. The restored Crowcombe Heathfield station, which features as the front cover of the 2002 book, is an outstanding example. Further examples of renovated stations are at Cranmore on the re-opened East Somerset Railway and Midsomer Norton South, where the Somerset & Dorset Railway Heritage Trust is intending to re-open a section of the former railway.

In a limited number of cases where the railway has gone, a complete set of the early station buildings has survived with the structures in new uses. The station building, goods shed and station master's house are still in place at Axbridge, Cheddar, Pylle, Sandford & Banwell and Venn Cross. In a number of other places the former station building is the principal survivor, the new uses being very varied. An excellent example is Bath Green Park where the wonderful train shed and building are now used for community uses and car parking, the latter associated with the adjacent Sainsbury's supermarket. A Homebase store covers a section of the former goods yard.

A number of station buildings have been converted into houses (for instance, Blagdon, Draycott, Evercreech Junction and Wellow); in many instances small or major extensions have been built. At Pill the former booking office and waiting room is now used by a building design firm and a baby supplies shop, whilst at Ilminster the station building is occupied by a pet parlour. An unusual example is that of the former Athelney station building, which, long after its closure in 1964, was cut into three sections and moved to Stoke St Gregory playing fields where it is now a sports pavilion.

A common feature in Somerset, as in many parts of the South West, is the continuing residential use of station masters' houses, exhibiting the architectural style of the appropriate railway company and adjacent station (eg bargeboards or ridge tiles). In some cases they stand in isolation close to the former station site which may now be in non residential use. However, there are a number of cases where they survive, standing out in their different styles in the heart of new housing development built on the site of the station and goods yard. In many cases their earlier role is revealed with the name 'Station House' but at some a non railway related name is given (eg Rose Villa), perhaps to deter railway enthusiasts from reaching for their camera!

Also surviving in residential use are examples of railway cottages constructed by the railway companies to house local railway workers such as signalmen, porters etc., again many of these are distinctive in the railway architectural style and the name 'Railway Cottages' still applies. Also surviving are a number of former goods sheds, the most common new use being as warehouses usually within an industrial estate developed on the whole former goods yard (eg Wookey Hole). At Cheddar the former shed has been converted into a large new house close to the station building now occupied by Wells Cathedral Stone Masons. At Ilminster the former shed is occupied by a carpet showroom and a firm of agricultural merchants.

Many of the sites, formerly occupied by the station itself and associated goods yards, today have considerable value for redevelopment located close to the heart of the settlements now much expanded compared to the early era of railway construction. As seen above, a number of these sites continue to contain railway related buildings but in many instances the site has been redeveloped with few or no remnants from the railway era. A wide variety of uses has taken over such sites; for example industrial/commercial development (eg Glastonbury and Street), housing (Wincanton), new roads (Burnham-on-Sea), a retail development (Clevedon) or a supermarket (Bridgwater North).

In researching these stations and goods yards, just as in industrial archaeology, the author discovered that, in almost every case, certain clues exist, even where no significant buildings remain. These clues include small sections of typical railway fencing, changes in the construction material on railway bridges where paths to a halt started or even derelict kissing gates where access paths left the road.

However, more substantial clues are also found, in particular the very common 'Station Road' which today serves no railway use whatever. Indeed, in one gazetteer relating to Somerset there are 55 Station Roads, the majority of which come in this category. An unusual example of marking the site of former Somerset stations is in the city of Wells, which was served at one time by three stations. The local Civic Society has erected stone plinths at the sites: 'East Somerset', 'Priory Road' and 'Tucker Street'. At Martock the boarded up 'Station Hotel' bears a plaque referring to the adjacent station site and

Draycott, where the station building has been converted into a house, preserving the name and decorative barge boards.

goods yard, now redeveloped as an industrial estate with only isolated remnants of former railway buildings and walls. This is also an example of public houses with names still related to the railway era. Unfortunately a number of these have, in recent years, been renamed, losing the references to the long gone railway. At Evercreech Junction the former Railway Hotel was first appropriately renamed 'The Silent Whistle' but is now called 'The Natterjack'!

During the 2010/2011 visits to the sites, photographs were taken of the current situation and many of them are reproduced here together with, as appropriate, historic photographs, generally illustrating the changes that have taken place over the years, as explained in the captions. Photographs are also included of other features that indicate the former presence of stations even where little or no trace now remains of the railway building (eg plinths, plaques and public house names).

At some former station sites there is today no feature of relevant photographic interest or it is impossible to take an appropriate comparison photograph and these cases are not illustrated in the book. In all cases however notes were made of the current situation at the sites and in the final section of the book a schedule sets out details of all Somerset's stations and halts: the dates of opening and closing of passenger and goods facilities, the grid reference of the site and a description of recent and current 2010/2011 uses. For further details regarding the dates when lines opened see also the following schedule 'Chronological Development of the Somerset Railways 1840 to 2011'. Maps also show the location of all the county's stations, including those on the Weston, Clevedon & Portishead Light Railway and the West Somerset Mineral Railway.

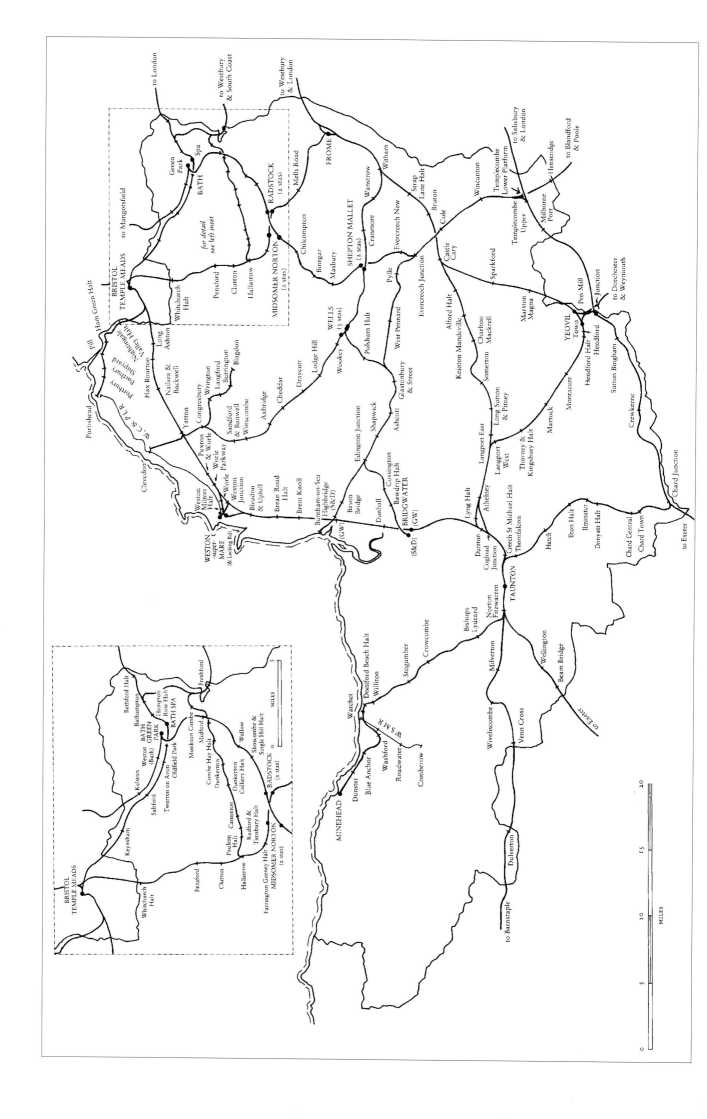

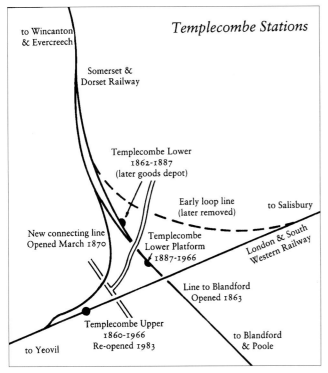

Templecombe Stations

to Wincanton & Evercreech

Somerset & Dorset Railway

Templecombe Lower
1862-1887
(later goods depot)

Early loop line
(later removed)

to Salisbury

New connecting line
Opened March 1870

Templecombe
Lower Platform
1887-1966

London & South
Western Railway

Line to Blandford
Opened 1863

Templecombe Upper
1860-1966
Re-opened 1983

to Yeovil

to Blandford
& Poole

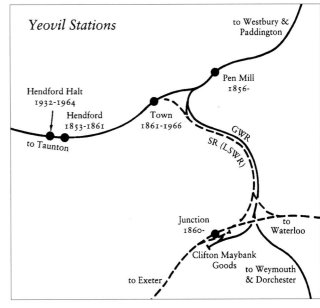

Yeovil Stations

to Westbury &
Paddington

Pen Mill
1856-

Hendford Halt
1932-1964

Hendford
1853-1861

Town
1861-1966

GWR

SR (LSWR)

to Taunton

Junction
1860-

to
Waterloo

Clifton Maybank
Goods

to Exeter

to Weymouth
& Dorchester

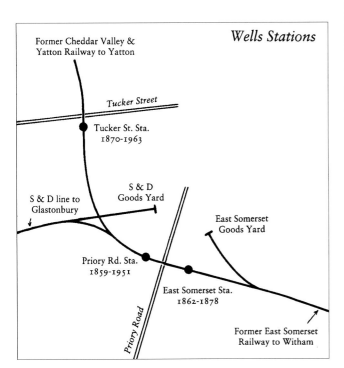

Wells Stations

Former Cheddar Valley &
Yatton Railway to Yatton

Tucker Street

Tucker St. Sta.
1870-1963

S & D
Goods Yard

S & D line to
Glastonbury

East Somerset
Goods Yard

Priory Rd. Sta.
1859-1951

East Somerset Sta.
1862-1878

Priory Road

Former East Somerset
Railway to Witham

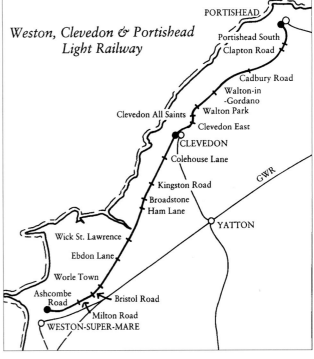

Weston, Clevedon & Portishead Light Railway

PORTISHEAD

Portishead South

Clapton Road

Cadbury Road

Walton-in-Gordano

Walton Park

Clevedon All Saints

Clevedon East

CLEVEDON

Colehouse Lane

Kingston Road

GWR

Broadstone

Ham Lane

YATTON

Wick St. Lawrence

Ebdon Lane

Worle Town

Ashcombe Road

Bristol Road

Milton Road

WESTON-SUPER-MARE

SOMERSET RAILWAYS

CHRONOLOGICAL DEVELOPMENT, 1840 – 2011

1840
31 August. Opening of the Bristol Temple Meads – Bath Spa section of the GWR Bristol to London line.

1841
14 June. Opening of the Bristol Temple Meads – Bridgwater section of the Bristol & Exeter Railway.

14 June. Opening of the Weston Junction – Weston-super-Mare branch from the Bristol & Exeter Railway.

30 June. Opening of the Bath Spa – Chippenham (via Box Tunnel) section of the GWR Bristol to London line.

1842
1 July. Opening of the Bridgwater – Taunton section of the Bristol & Exeter Railway.

1843
1 May. Opening of the Taunton – Beam Bridge (temporary rail-head SW of Wellington) section of the Bristol & Exeter Railway.

1844
1 May. Opening of the Beam Bridge – Exeter section of the Bristol & Exeter Railway.

1847
28 July. Opening of the Yatton – Clevedon branch from the Bristol & Exeter Railway.

1850
7 October. Opening of the Westbury (Wilts) – Frome section of the Wilts, Somerset & Weymouth Railway.

1853
1 October. Opening of the Durston – Hendford (Yeovil) branch from the Bristol & Exeter Railway to passenger traffic. Subsequently extended to Yeovil Pen Mill on the Wilts, Somerset & Weymouth Railway on 2 February 1857.

26 October. Opening of the Durston – Hendford (Yeovil) branch to goods traffic.

1854.
28 August. Opening of the Highbridge Wharf – Glastonbury section of the Somerset Central Railway.

14 November. Opening of the Frome – Radstock branch from the Wilts, Somerset & Weymouth Railway for coal traffic.

1856
1 September. Opening of the Frome – Yeovil Pen Mill section of the Wilts, Somerset & Weymouth Railway.

1857
20 January. Opening of the Yeovil – Dorchester section of the Wilts, Somerset & Weymouth Railway.

2 February. Opening of the Bathampton – Bradford Junction section of the Wilts, Somerset & Weymouth Railway.

1858
3 May. Opening of the Highbridge – Burnham-on-Sea extension of the Somerset Central Railway.

9 November. Opening of the Witham – Shepton Mallet section of the East Somerset Railway.

1859
15 March. Opening of the Glastonbury – Wells branch from the Somerset Central Railway.

2 May. Opening of the Salisbury – Gillingham section of the Salisbury & Yeovil Railway.

28 September. Opening to public goods traffic of the West Somerset Mineral Railway.

1860
7 May. Opening of the Gillingham – Sherborne section of the Salisbury & Yeovil Railway.

1 June. Opening of the Sherborne – Yeovil (Hendford) section of the Salisbury & Yeovil Railway.

19 July. Opening of the Yeovil Junction – Exeter section of the London & South Western Railway.

1862
3 February. Opening of the Cole – Templecombe section of the Dorset Central Railway and opening of the Glastonbury – Cole section of the Somerset Central Railway.

1 March. Opening of the Shepton Mallet – Wells section of the East Somerset Railway.

31 March. Opening of the West Somerset Railway from Norton Fitzwarren (on the Bristol to Exeter line) – Watchet.

1863
8 May. Opening of the Chard Junction – Chard Town branch from the Salisbury to Exeter line.

10 September. Opening of the Blandford St Mary – Blandford – Templecombe section of the Somerset & Dorset Railway.

1865
4 September. Opening of the Watchet – Comberow section of the West Somerset Mineral Railway to passenger traffic.

1866
11 September. Opening of the Taunton – Chard Joint branch from the Bristol to Exeter line.

1867

18 April. Opening of the Portishead branch from the Bristol to Exeter line.

1869

3 August. Opening of the Yatton – Cheddar section of the Cheddar Valley & Yatton Railway.

4 August. Opening of the Mangotsfield (Gloucestershire) – Bath branch from the Bristol to Gloucester line.

1870

5 April. Opening of the Cheddar – Wells section of the Cheddar Valley & Yatton Railway.

1871

8 June. Opening of the Norton Fitzwarren – Wiveliscombe section of the Devon & Somerset Railway.

1873

3 September. Opening of the Bristol & North Somerset Railway, Bristol – Radstock.

1 November. Opening of the Wiveliscombe – Barnstaple section of the Devon & Somerset Railway.

1874

16 July. Opening of the Minehead Railway, Minehead – Watchet.

20 July. Opening of the Bath Extension of the Somerset & Dorset Railway, Evercreech Junction to Bath.

1875

5 July. Opening of the Radstock – Frome line to passenger traffic.

1878

1 January. First GWR trains run over the section in Wells of the Somerset & Dorset Railway between the original Cheddar Valley & Yatton and East Somerset Railways.

1882

1 March. Opening of the Hallatrow – Camerton branch from the Bristol & North Somerset Railway to goods traffic. Opening to passenger traffic one month later on 1 April.

1884

1 March. Opening of the Weston-super-Mare loop line and closure of the spur line from Weston Junction to Weston-super-Mare.

1890

21 July. Opening of the Bridgwater branch of the Somerset & Dorset Railway from Edington Junction to Bridgwater North.

1897

1 December. Opening of the Weston-super-Mare – Clevedon section of the Weston – Clevedon – Portishead Light Railway.

1898

7 November. Closure of the West Somerset Mineral Railway to passenger and mineral traffic.

1901

4 December. Opening of the Wrington Vale Light Railway, Congresbury – Blagdon.

1905

1 July. Opening of the Castle Cary – Charlton Mackrell section of the GWR southern cut off route (Castle Cary – Cogload Junction).

1906

12 February. Opening of the Curry Rivel Junction – Somerton section of the GWR cut off for goods traffic.

2 April. Opening of the Athelney – Cogload Junction section of the cut off at first for goods traffic only.

20 May. Opening of the Charlton Mackrell – Somerton section of the cut off route, at first for local goods traffic only.

2 July. Opening of the GWR cut off route from Castle Cary – Cogload Junction for through passenger traffic.

1907

4 July. Re-opening of the West Somerset Mineral Railway for mineral traffic only. Also limited passenger service until 1910.

7 August. Opening of the Clevedon – Portishead section of the Weston – Clevedon – Portishead Light Railway.

1910

9 May. Opening of the Camerton – Limpley Stoke (Cam Valley) line linking the Bristol & North Somerset branch line at Camerton with the Wilts, Somerset & Weymouth Railway.

1915

22 March –9 July 1923. Temporary closure of the Hallatrow – Limpley Stoke line to passenger traffic. Closure to goods traffic as from 1 April 1918.

1925

21 September. Closure of the Hallatrow – Limpley Stoke line to passenger traffic.

1931

14 September. Closure of the Wrington Vale Light Railway to passenger traffic.

1940

18 May. Closure of the Weston-super-Mare – Clevedon – Portishead Light Railway.

1950

1 November. Closure of Wrington Vale Light Railway, Wrington – Blagdon section to goods traffic.

1951

3 February – 7 May. Temporary closure to all traffic of the Taunton – Chard Junction line during the fuel crisis.

15 February. Hallatrow – Limpley Stoke line closed entirely.

29 October. Closure of Highbridge – Burnham-on-Sea line to passenger services.

29 October. Closure of the Wells branch.

1952

1 December. Closure of Bridgwater North branch of Somerset & Dorset to passenger traffic.

1954

4 October. Closure of Bridgwater North branch of Somerset & Dorset to goods traffic.

1959

2 November. Bristol – Radstock – Frome closed to passenger traffic.

1962

10 September. Closure of Taunton – Chard Junction line.

10 September. Withdrawal of local passenger services Castle Cary – Taunton.

1963

10 June. Congresbury – Wrington section of the Wrington Vale Light Railway closed completely.

10 June. Yatton – Clevedon closed to goods traffic.

9 September. Closure of the Yatton – Witham line to passenger traffic.

1964

15 June. Closure of Taunton – Yeovil line to passenger traffic.

6 July. Closure of Taunton – Yeovil line to all traffic.

3 August. Closure of the Norton Fitzwarren – Wiveliscombe – Barnstaple line to freight traffic.

7 September. Closure of Portishead branch to passenger traffic.

1 October. Closure of Yatton – Witham line to freight traffic.

1966

7 March. Closure of the Bath Green Park – Poole line to passenger traffic.

7 March. Closure of the Evercreech Junction – Highbridge line to passenger traffic.

3 October. Closure of the Barnstaple line, Norton Fitzwarren – Barnstaple.

3 October. Yatton – Clevedon branch closed to passenger traffic.

1967

1 May. Closure of Portishead branch to public goods traffic.

1968

11 July. Bristol – Radstock closed to goods traffic.

1971

4 January. Closure of Minehead line, Norton Fitzwarren – Minehead.

31 May. Final closure of Mangotsfield – Bath Green Park line to all traffic.

1972

3 October. Closure of Highbridge – Bason Bridge for milk traffic.

1976

28 March. Re-opening of Minehead – Blue Anchor section of restored West Somerset Railway.

28 August. West Somerset Railway extended from Blue Anchor – Williton.

1978

7 May. Re-opening of Williton – Stogumber section of West Somerset Railway.

1979

9 June. Re-opening of Stogumber – Bishops Lydeard section of West Somerset Railway.

1980

4 April. Services commenced on East Somerset Railway, Cranmore – Merryfield Lane.

1981

3 April. Portishead branch closed to all goods traffic.

1992

East Somerset Railway, extended from Merryfield Lane to Mendip Vale.

2001

21 December. Portishead branch re-opened in part to traffic serving the Royal Portbury Dock.

THE STATIONS AND HALTS

ATHELNEY

TOP The main station building at the west end of the down (towards Taunton) platform on 8th December 1963.

MIDDLE The re-erected building, purchased for £25, in use as a sports pavilion at Stoke St Gregory playing fields on 27th August 2010.

LEFT The station master's house continuing in residential use 'Old Station House' on 27th August, close to the now automatic level crossing.

ABOVE The station building and platform in the late 1950s. Note the fine barge boards, the plain and patterned roof tiles and the cruciform style ridge tiles.

LEFT The building in use as Axbridge Youth Centre on 20th May 2010. The A371 road runs alongside, level with the now grass covered platform.

BELOW LEFT The goods shed in the late 1950s with fine barge boards and a canopy over the two road side doors.

BELOW The shed, now in commercial use at the end of Station Road on 20th May 2010. The barge boards and canopy survive.

BASON BRIDGE

Looking west at the platform and wooden buildings on 10th June 1960.

Just over 50 years later, on 19th July 2010, the east end and ramp of the platform can just be seen in the undergrowth.

BATH GREEN PARK (1)

The fine glazed train shed on 2nd June 1963. Trains to the south coast on the Somerset & Dorset Railway departed from the long platform (right). To the left is the bonded warehouse, which does not survive today.

Some 47 years later on 10th December 2010, the restored train shed is used for car parking and retail uses. To the right is the recently extended Sainsbury's store.

The Bath stone front elevation in the late 19th century. An iron and glass canopy protects passengers entering and leaving the building. A horse drawn carriage waits for passengers.

Over a century later on 10th December 2010, a view of the renovated elevation and canopy. A door has been created (left) through the single storey section giving access to the train shed retail units and Sainsbury's.

An early view looking west through the glazed train shed. A train stands at the arrival platform (right). Spare carriages and trucks occupy central tracks. Passengers await a train on the departure platform (left) for services to the south coast on the Somerset & Dorset Railway.

From a similar viewpoint over 100 years later on 10th December 2010. Parked cars stand under the restored glazed train shed. Retail units and stalls occupy the former departure platform (left), many displaying Christmas gifts.

BATH SPA

The northern frontage in about 1899. Horse drawn carriages wait for passengers.

On 13th May 2010 the frontage is largely unchanged, but the transport is very different.

On 28th August 1958 the down Paddington to Weston-super-Mare 'Merchant Venturer' hauled by 4-6-0 No 6003 King George IV stands beside the down platform. The 1897 elevated signal box, above the canopy, closed 10 years later.

Over 50 years later on 13th May 2010, the only significant changes are the absence of the elevated signal box and the two central tracks removed in November 1962 and March 1967.

BINEGAR

Looking south-east on 18th May 1963. To the left of the main building the adjoining houses occupied by the station master (or agent) and signalman can just be seen.

On 1st July 2010 the station site is occupied by a large house, 'The Beechings'. The surviving adjoining houses are seen centre left and to their left is the former goods shed now converted to residential use.

BISHOPS LYDEARD

Looking south in June 1966 at the main station building on the down (towards Minehead) platform. Beyond is the large goods shed and the station master's house.

From the same viewpoint on 5th August 2010. The station, now on the restored West Somerset Railway, shows some changes including a new structure for the Taunton Model Railway Group between the original building and the goods shed. The West Somerset Railway Association shop and buffet is beyond the original shelter on the up platform (left).

An early view looking east prior to a 1920s extension of the building at its west end. Note the cast iron gent's urinal.

From a similar viewpoint on 8th March 2011, an old guards' van stands behind the platform and behind the surviving station building is a two storey building constructed in the 1960s, including stonework from the demolished Worle (near Weston-super-Mare) station. The original wooden building and the 1960s structure, linked by a single storey section, now form a substantial family house 'Little Halt'.

BLEADON AND UPHILL

The up (towards Bristol) platform in about 1910. The central shelter and the station master's house (top right) date from the early Bristol & Exeter Railway era.

A view of the former station site on 17th August 2010 from the A370 road bridge. The garden was the site of a railway museum in the 1970s and 1980s. The former station master's house with extensions continues in residential use.

BLUE ANCHOR

Looking east in about 1910 at the original 1874 platform and building. Beyond the building is the 1904 ladies' room. The down (towards Minehead) platform (right), added in 1904, serves the later passing loop.

On 5th August 2010 the 1500 hrs Minehead to Bishops Lydeard train waits at the up platform for a train to Minehead. The only change to the buildings, now operated by the West Somerset Railway, is a 1989 shelter between the building and the ladies' room.

BRIDGWATER

Looking north in 1934 at the Brunel design 1840s Grade II listed buildings. Note the fine covered footbridge and the glazed screen at the south end of the up platform (left) canopy. A large corrugated iron structure with a clerestory roof contains cloakroom and parcel storage facilities. The large Railway Hotel dominates the skyline.

Some 75 years later on 24th May 2010, a Cross Country train from Taunton en route to Edinburgh rushes through. The corrugated iron structure has gone and a garage has replaced the Railway Hotel.

BRIDGWATER NORTH

Looking south at the terminus station in about 1960. The main building is at right angles to the tracks. Note the tall tower of St John's Church (right).

From about the same viewpoint some 50 years later on 24th May 2010, the pinnacles on the church tower confirming the same angle of view. The site is almost totally in use for car parking at the Sainsbury's store just off to the right of the picture.

BRUTON

Looking west on 27th October 1962, substantial stone buildings on both platforms. The main building incorporating the station offices is on the up (towards Frome) platform (right). The gardens and bushes are well tended.

Again looking west nearly 50 years later on 8th July 2010 as a High Speed Train from Paddington to the West Country passes through at speed. Only trains on the Bristol to Weymouth services stop at Bruton. The renovated facilities are kept in good condition by the Friends of Bruton Station.

BURNHAM-ON-SEA

LEFT Looking west, towards the sea front, at the station building with its overall roof, the large goods shed and the small signal box (left to right). Above the station roof, in the far distance, is the Queens Hotel.

BELOW LEFT From a viewpoint on Marine Drive, which covers the former trackbed, the hotel survives on the corner of the sea front and Pier Street. The station building stood on the extreme right.

LEFT The small signal box shown above is now at the Somerset & Dorset Railway Trust's display at Washford on the West Somerset Railway.

BURRINGTON

LEFT Looking east in 1925 at the 1907 stone building and platform on the south side of the Wrington Vale Light Railway.

BELOW Looking west at the closed (1931) station in 1949. Dominating the skyline is the station master's house south of the road bridge.

The station house with the station master and his wife at Christmas 1912.

'Station House' now with a large extension, just under a century later, on 27th May 2010.

Looking west on 26th April 1970, the main building on the up (towards Westbury) platform (right) and the original 1856 shelter on the single face down platform (left). In the far distance is the 1954/55 goods shed and the white ARP 1942 signal box, both replacing earlier structures destroyed or damaged in a September 1942 air raid.

The 1222 hrs train en route from Weymouth to Bristol and Gloucester stands at the now two face island platform on 5th July 2010. The train (with the author on board!) is about to pass beneath the footbridge before switching to the main up line en route to Westbury. Note the 1984 concrete hut that has replaced the 1856 shelter on the down platform. The 1942 signal box has gone and the goods shed (centre top) is unused. Posters erected in late June for the Glastonbury Festival visitors remain in place (see bottom left).

CHARD CENTRAL

TOP A train en route from Taunton to Chard Junction stands at the platform with its carriages beneath the overall wooden train shed in about 1960, some two years before closure to passenger services.

ABOVE A view of the station from the approach road on 8th August 1962, only 5 months before closure to passenger services.

LEFT A similar view of the now redundant building nearly 50 years later on 24th June 2010. At that time it was unused but previous inspection showed it had been used as a tyre depot (1994) and by engine parts and international shipping firms (2002).

CHARD JUNCTION

LEFT Looking up (towards Yeovil) through the fine covered footbridge connecting the platforms on the main Yeovil to Exeter line. The principal building is on the up platform (left). Only a section of this platform survives today.

BELOW Looking east at the separate branch (from Taunton) platform and station forecourt. To the right is the principal building on the up main platform. In the distance, beyond the forecourt, is the Three Counties Hotel.

LEFT From a similar viewpoint on 24th June 2010. The only surviving building is the Three Counties Hotel, now providing en suite accommodation. Remains of the branch platform are in the coalyard to the left of the picture.

CHARD TOWN

The former station in use as a goods depot in 1962. Old sleepers separate different materials on the platform.

From about the same viewpoint on 24th June 2010. The sole surviving building compared with the earlier photograph is the house on East Street (centre), seen to the right of the goods truck in the 1962 view. Tapstone Road and the filling station cover the site of the former station and goods depot.

CHARLTON MACKRELL

Looking west on 10th April 1962, exactly 5 months before the station's closure. Standard Class 3MT 2-6-2T calls with the 0855 hrs Taunton to Castle Cary stopping train.

The station buildings and platforms have gone on 27th August 2010. The Charltons Community Hall stands on the site of the down (towards Taunton) side of the station. Apart from the sign 'Station Road' no other remnant of the railway era survives.

CHEDDAR

ABOVE Looking east at the overall wooden train shed on 23rd June 1953. To the left is the station building with typical Bristol & Exeter Railway barge boards.

LEFT The west end of the former station building occupied by the Wells Cathedral Stone Masons on 20th May 2010. One of the columns supporting the original train shed survives, as do the house barge boards.

BELOW LEFT The station master's house continuing in residential use 'Station House' on Wideatts Road.

BELOW The former goods shed now converted into a fine house on Old Station Close, photographed on 20th May 2010.

CHILCOMPTON

TOP A close up of the main building on the down platform containing a general waiting room, ladies' waiting room, booking office and station master's office.

ABOVE A view from the west in 1959, the main building with its sloping canopy on the down platform (right) and a wooden shelter with canopy on the up (towards Radstock).

LEFT From a similar viewpoint some 50 years later on 29th August 2010, the road, Station Mead (the only road of that name in Somerset) is on the approximate alignment of the former Somerset & Dorset Railway trackbed. Note the house above the car in the distance can also be seen in the 1959 photograph.

CLEVEDON

ABOVE A general view looking north of the station as remodelled in 1890. The original 1847 train shed covers the platform at the buffers end. Note the massive water tower.

RIGHT From the same viewpoint on 9th December 2010, showing the rear of retail units in the Triangle Centre which covers much of the station site. The hill ridge line in the background is similar to that in the earlier photo.

LOWER RIGHT The station frontage and forecourt in 1949. Note the distinctive building on Kenn Road to the right of the photograph.

LEFT A view on 17th April 2010 from under a metal canopy on the east side of the Triangle Centre. The distinctive building on Kenn Road remains, now the Clevedon Conservative Club. The church tower on the horizon can just be glimpsed to the right of the station's central chimney in the 1949 photo.

CLUTTON

Looking south with the principal building on the up (towards Bristol) side (right), a fine example of the standard Bristol & North Somerset Railway design by the architect William Clarke. All the buildings shown have now gone and there is a housing development on the southern half of the former lower goods yard.

On Station Road above the station site, 'The Railway' public house is seen on 1st July 2010.

COLE

Looking north in 1962 with the main building of typical Dorset Central Railway style on the down platform (right).

On 8th July 2010 the former main building (left) and station master's house both now in residential use on Old Station Lane that provides access to 1990s housing development on the former goods yard.

CONGRESBURY

Looking north at the down platform and buildings in 1952/53 with the goods shed to the right and the bridge carrying the A370 over the line to the left.

From a similar viewpoint on 28th March 2011, the Strawberry Line Trail follows the former trackbed between sections of the platforms which survive in the vegetation. In the foreground is a wooden seat and table manufactured from material saved from the redevelopment of Weston-super-Mare Grand Pier following the 2008 fire.

COSSINGTON

The station building with canopy is dominated by the station master's two storey house. The ground frame hut beside the house has been transferred to the East Somerset Railway at Cranmore.

A view on 19th July 2010 showing the road side of the former station master's house, now in residential use as 'Old Station House' (left) and 'Station Cottage', the former station building..

CRANMORE

TOP Looking east towards Witham with the main building and gent's cast iron urinal on the up platform (left). A small wooden shelter serves passengers on the down (towards Shepton Mallet) platform.

CENTRE Again looking east on 22nd August 2010 with the surviving main building and urinal on the former up platform (left). Beyond the main building is a 1974 house. To the right the unused down side platform is covered in grass.

LEFT The 1991 building housing the Whistlestop Café on the ground floor with a shop and booking office on the floor above. Material for the building came from the demolished Lodge Hill Station and Wells Priory Road goods shed.

Staff pose in front of the fine William Tite design building on the up (towards Yeovil) platform. The principal station offices are in the single storey section beyond the three storey station master's house. Note the covered footbridge and the original wooden signal box.

A view on 24th June 2010 of the renovated station building. The tall former station master's house section is occupied by a firm of accountants. The footbridge has gone.

CROWCOMBE HEATHFIELD

Looking east on 14th April 1968 with the main station building (extreme left) and the stone built goods shed, demolished when goods traffic ceased in 1964, on the up platform. On the down platform (right) is the original wooden waiting shelter and 1867 signal box.

A view from the north end of the up platform in use on the restored West Somerset Railway on 12th August 2010. To the left is the much renovated main building. On the down platform is the 1996 wooden shelter and the replacement signal box, which operated from 1994.

DONYATT HALT

The halt on 14th April 1962, the single platform is faced with wooden sleepers. Passengers are served by a small wooden hut.

The reconstructed halt alongside the 'Stop Line' cycle and pedestrian way on 24th June 2010, the name reflecting its alignment along the line of concrete traps between the English and Bristol Channels, examples of which are seen above the halt. Alongside the hut is a small statue of Doreen, a local war-time evacuee, whose story is told on the board mounted on the hut wall.

DRAYCOTT

On 15th March 1963 a train from Yatton to Frome arrives at the platform. Above the platform door are the words 'Draycott Station', the splendid barge boards are also a feature. Beyond the small signal box is the station master's house.

The former station building and station house viewed from Station Road, both in residential use on 2nd January 2011. The former's barge boards survive and the cruciform ridge tiles are still in situ.

DULVERTON

A general view towards Taunton on 20th August 1953. The large station master's house and single storey station offices are on the up platform (left). A train stands at the inner face of the island platform.

A view from the B3222 across extensive gardens of the renovated main station building and goods shed (right), both in residential use on 12th August 2010.

DUNSTER

Looking east, in the British Rail era, at the station building and goods shed on 30th October 1965, just over 6 years before closure to passengers.

Little has changed some 45 years later at the reopened station (28.3.1976) on the restored West Somerset Railway. Both the station building and goods shed are listed Grade II. Much renovation and restoration has been undertaken on both structures seen here on 12th August 2010.

EDINGTON BURTLE

ABOVE Looking west in 1933 at the station then known as Edington Junction. A train from the Bridgwater branch is approaching the bay platform on the south side of the island (left). A wooden shelter with a sloping canopy serves passengers on the down (towards Evercreech Junction) platform (right).

LEFT A small section of the former island platform midst extensive brambles and undergrowth on 19th July 2010.

RIGHT The current sign at the 'Tom Mogg Inn', north-east of the station site, named after a former signalman/porter at the station. An earlier sign had more appropriately shown Tom Mogg with a former Somerset Central Railway hand bell at the level crossing.

BELOW The extensively extended and modernised former station master's house on 19th July 2010.

TOP Looking north-west on 18th May 1963, the two storey station master's house (right) and the single storey station building (centre) on the down platform. A water pump stands between the tracks.

ABOVE AND LEFT The former station building and the station master's house in residential use on 1st July 2010.

A 1949 view of the halt which had one of the smallest shelters on any Somerset station.

Looking in the opposite direction after the halt has closed and the shelter gone. At the end of the bridge is the Miners Arms public house at which tickets were purchased from a small window.

LEFT AND BELOW The Miners Arms ticket office window in 1949 (left) and the surviving original window with explanatory notice on the wall of the now 'Spice Dunes Indian Restaurant'.

ABOVE The 1860 first station with the main building on the up (towards Bristol) side. The access path, behind the signal box, climbs up the side of the cutting to a point near the station master's house which survives today on Clevedon Road. The high footbridge over the mixed gauge line (right) also survives.

ABOVE Again looking towards Bristol as No 6975 pulls a down train in 1959 through the 1893 second station with the main building on the up platform and the goods shed (left). The footbridge is of a standard GWR design of the late 19th/early 20th century.

LEFT The house name displayed on the gate of the station master's house linked to the first station, photographed on 30th September 2010.

FRESHFORD

Looking towards Bath in June 1963. Attractive buildings with small canopies serve passengers on both platforms. A fine covered footbridge connects the platforms, unusual for a relatively small station. Well kept gardens are a feature.

From an almost identical viewpoint nearly 50 years later on 17th July 2010. Modern metal and glass shelters and new lamps are in place as well as a new open footbridge.

FROME

Looking north at the station building including the fine wooden train shed in October 1962. Beyond the shed the platform canopy that protected passengers on the main up (towards Westbury) and bay platforms can be seen.

Looking north on 5th July 2010 at the surviving Grade II listed train shed. Only the former up platform (left) remains in use by trains on the Bristol to Weymouth services and peak hour services to and from London.

TOP Looking north-west into the station from close to Dyehouse Lane on 29th August 1964. To the left are large saw mills. The island platform is to the right, note the fine covered footbridge.

ABOVE From a similar viewpoint on 19th July 2010. Note the renovated level crossing gates. The metal plates across the centre of the picture originally carried the tracks over a stream into the station.

LEFT The re-erected island platform canopy at St Johns Car Park in the town centre also on 19th July 2010. The scheme was awarded 2nd prize in a national 'Pride of Place' competition in 1984.

HALLATROW

Looking north as passengers and staff pose on the down (towards Radstock) platform. The fine local stone building with its large horizontal canopy is typical of those on the stations of the Bristol & North Somerset Railway. The design by William Clarke is also found at many other stations in the West Country.

The main building renovated and extended as a fine house, 'The Ticket Office', on 19th January 2011. The large extension has been built on the former trackbed.

LEFT AND BELOW 'The Old Station' public house on the A39 south of the station with an old railway carriage acting as a restaurant in the rear garden on 19th January 2011.

HATCH

Looking south in about 1959 at the main station building with the goods shed beyond.

The station building and goods shed both in use by a stone/masonry firm on 24th June 2010.

HENSTRIDGE

Looking north towards Templecombe in July 1961. The wooden station building is at the smallest station on the Somerset & Dorset line from Bath to Poole. The road over bridge in the far distance carries the A30 over the single track line.

From a similar viewpoint on 21st October 2010. The gravel path (right) follows the former trackbed towards the surviving A30 road bridge (far distance). The station site in the foreground is now grass covered.

Looking north on 29th August 1964, impressive buildings with horizontal canopies on both platforms. A concrete footbridge, which replaced an earlier covered structure connects the two platforms. An eastern extension links to the adjacent Somerset & Dorset station which is behind the bush on the right of the picture.

Again looking north on 19th July 2010 as a late morning Cross Country train from Manchester to Paignton speeds through en route to Taunton. Modern metal and glass shelters have replaced the original buildings on both platforms but the concrete footbridge, minus the eastern extension, remains.

HIGHBRIDGE EAST (S & D)

Looking east over the station in 1933 with a train at the terminus platform 1. In the distance is the Highbridge works of the Somerset & Dorset Railway. To the right is a glimpse of the concrete footbridge which also crosses the main Bristol to Taunton line at Highbridge and Burnham station.

A complete transformation in this view across the former station site on 19th July 2010. It was taken from the concrete footbridge which now only links the platforms at the north end of the open Highbridge and Burnham station. The extension to the Somerset & Dorset station has gone. A large housing development now covers the station site, access roads include Somerset Way and Dorset Close.

ILMINSTER

Looking south towards Chard in about 1959. Beyond the single face platform is the goods shed. Note the horizontal all round canopy, a typical feature of stations on the Taunton to Chard line.

The station building on the road side on 24th June 2010, occupied by the 'Glamour Pets' parlour. Beyond the station is the goods shed, now occupied by a carpet showroom and a firm of .agricultural merchants.

KELSTON

Looking south-east at the station in 1949, the main building (left) being on the down (towards Bath) platform.

From a similar viewpoint on 2nd March 2011, the trackbed now used by the Bristol – Bath Cycleway.

A west facing view in about 1909. The fine covered footbridge, bearing the emblem of the GWR, was dismantled in 1970 and subsequently re-erected at Buckfastleigh on the South Devon Railway. The substantial buildings on both platforms were demolished in the same year.

From a similar viewpoint over 100 years later on 26th May 2010. The replacement footbridge has ramped steps connecting to the up platform (right) but only standard steps link to the down. Beyond the footbridge shelters dating from the 1930s survive. A brick shelter from a major re-vamp of 1985 serves passengers, some of whom will have left their cars in the expanded car park behind the platform (far right).

LANGPORT EAST

A steam rail motor arriving from Castle Cary in about 1910. The main building is on the down platform (right).

The limited surviving remains of the station in Eastover Road on 27th August 2010. Bottom right is a section of the base of the down platform building and above this is a small section of the railings that once ran behind the platform.

LANGPORT WEST

The station looking north in about 1910 with staff posing on the platform and between the tracks. Note the road bridge carrying the A378 over the line.

From a similar viewpoint, now in the Westover Trading Estate, some 100 years later on 27th August 2010. The road bridge is still there though the slightly different arch suggests it has been modified or rebuilt at some point.

The station on the single line looking west in the 1960s. Note the distinctive Bristol & Exeter Railway style barge boards and cruciform style ridge tiles. Materials from the demolished building were used subsequently in the construction of the new building at Cranmore on the restored East Somerset Railway. Beyond the station building the goods shed can be seen.

Again looking west from the surviving road over bridge. The station building has gone but the goods shed is, on 20th May 2010, within the Lodge Hill Business Park.

BELOW Two views of the goods shed - in railway use in the 1960s with the goods office closest to the camera and on 20th May 2010 in commercial use, including the Business Park office.

LONG SUTTON AND PITNEY

Looking west in the late 1950s from the Hermitage Road bridge that spans the cutting carrying the line between Castle Cary and Taunton via Cogload Junction. Today only a section of the former down platform (left) remains at trackside.

The station master's house on the east side of Hermitage Road south of the road bridge on 27th August 2010. It continues in residential use, 'Station House'.

MARSTON MAGNA

Looking south towards Yeovil on 1st October 1966, two days before the station closed to passengers. Only a section of the railings behind the down platform (left) between the station master's house (extreme left) and the main building survives today.

On 24th July 2010 a view south of the former station site from the bridge carrying Rimpton Road over the now single track line. The station master's house, with extensions, continues in residential use, 'Chartwell House' (left). Behind the house is a surviving section of platform railings.

A view in about 1912 of the station showing the forecourt, road side of the main building on the down platform, the approach road, the signal box and the level crossing gate across Stapleton Road.

From about the same viewpoint on 24th July 2010 at the junction of Stapleton Road and Coat Road. Industrial units on the Martock Business Park cover the station site.

To the left of the viewpoint of the July 2010 photo was the derelict former Railway Hotel on which this plaque is displayed..

MIDFORD

Looking north towards Bath in 1951. At that time the station building still had an attractive canopy.

Some 60 years later on 3rd September 2010 looking north along what is now a section of the National Cycle Network route No 24 laid on the former trackbed. The southern ramp of the platform in the photo above is to the left of the gate behind the public house car park notice.

Looking west with the main building, a good example of the William Clarke design used on the Bristol & North Somerset Railway that incorporates a large horizontal canopy and three tall chimneys.

From about the same viewpoint on 29th August 2010, now at the west end of the new metal bridge that carries the National Cycle Network route No 48 over Station Road. The station has completely gone but the cycleway (left) follows the line of the former trackbed.

Looking south on 18th May 1963 showing the main building on the down (towards Radstock) platform, the up side shelter, the signal box and greenhouse.

From an almost identical viewpoint on 29th August 2010, a view of the site now run by the Somerset & Dorset Railway Heritage Trust. The photo shows the restored main building and shelter, the rebuilt signal box and the greenhouse which, at that time, was being reconstructed.

BELOW Two views showing the goods shed in operation in 1951 and functioning as a restoration workshop on 29th August 2010.

MINEHEAD (THEN)

LEFT The west end of the main station building some years before the 1920s extension. This was built over the site of the GWR pagoda style hut seen here which was providing extra shelter. A number of horse drawn carriages stand waiting for passengers.

BELOW A general view looking west, on 30th October 1965, including the 1934 canopy (centre) and the goods shed. North Hill rises in the background.

LEFT The south road side frontage in about 1970. The view includes the major western extension of the building (this side of the parked car) completed in the 1920s and the large 200 ft long platform canopy added in 1934 (right).

MINEHEAD (NOW)

RIGHT The west end of the main building on 5th August 2010. A booking office has been added to the 1920s extended station, incorporating fittings from Cardiff General (now Central) station.

BELOW Looking along the main platform with a West Somerset Railway train from Bishops Lydeard standing at the platform (right). In this view of 5th August 2010 the new turntable and Turntable Cafe are to the left of the large canopy, an engine is on the former.

RIGHT A view on 5th August 2010 of the road side frontage. Note the recently renovated large platform canopy (centre) and the Turntable Café (right) opened in 2009.

ABOVE The station looking west on 28th August 1950 some 4 months before it closed completely. Passenger services had ceased 25 years earlier. Beyond the truck are level crossing gates where the line to Camerton crosses Mill Lane. The station entrance is to the right of the gates.

LEFT The entrance to Monkton Combe station on 23rd June 1952 as modified by a film company shooting 'The Titfield Thunderbolt'. Note the two gateposts.

On 3rd September 2010 the sole remnants of the station are the two gateposts now either side of a garage on the east side of Mill Lane. Close by is No 1 Station Cottages. The station site is buried beneath the raised sports field of Monkton Combe School.

TOP A Taunton to Yeovil train arrives at the station in 1963, a year before it closed to passengers.

CENTRE A standard class 3MT No 82042 stands at the station on 18th May 1964 with a Taunton to Yeovil train. To the right of the train is the station master's house.

RIGHT Looking north along the A3088 some 46 years later on 24th July 2010, the road is along the former trackbed. The car stands at the entrance to the station master's house. The station has completely gone.

TOP Staff pose in front of the impressive Brunel design structure on the up (towards Bristol) platform with its bay windows. Apart from a short central section the platform is constructed of timber because of its embankment siting.

CENTRE A general view looking west showing the Bristol & Exeter Railway era wooden shelter on the down platform (left).

BOTTOM Again from the footbridge on 28th September 2010 as the 1151 hrs Cross Country service from Taunton to Glasgow rushes through. Metal and glass shelters serve passengers on both platforms..

OLDFIELD PARK

TOP A view towards Bath in 1951, two corrugated iron shelters provide cover on each platform. The photographer's wife and child posing as a foreground?

CENTRE On 20th August 1961 a Sunday morning Bristol to Weymouth train enters the station hauled by 4-6-0 No 1014 County of Glamorgan. The arc roofed corrugated iron shelter serves passengers on the down platform (left), in the foreground is a hut with a ventilator roof containing the gentlemen's and ladies' toilets.

BOTTOM From the same viewpoint almost 50 years later on 7th March 2011 the 1500 hrs Bristol Temple Meads to Paddington train passes through at speed. Two modern metal and glass shelters are now provided for passengers to Bristol.

PENSFORD

Passengers and staff pose in this early view of the station looking south. The main building is in the style of William Clarke, the architect of other stations on the Bristol & North Somerset Railway and also many other station buildings in the West Country. The whole site, including the goods yard south of the station, has been redeveloped for housing accessed by the road, 'Station Approach'.

The station master's house behind the main building on Station Approach continues in residential use, 'Station House', surrounded by modern houses.

PILL

A steam rail motor from Portishead to Bristol enters the up platform in about 1910. Brick shelters serve passengers on both platforms which are sited within a wide cutting in the heart of the village.

Looking north-west again from the road bridge some 100 years later on 16th August 2010. The up platform edge (right) can clearly be seen alongside the single track line now serving Royal Portbury Dock. In the far distance is the bridge carrying the M5 motorway across the River Avon.

PORTBURY

A train stands at the station en route to Portishead in 1961. The impressive building incorporated the main station offices and accommodation for the station master. The view is taken from a bridge carrying Station Road over the single track line.

From the same viewpoint some 50 years later on 16th August 2010, the building in residential use. A single rusty track is hidden beneath the undergrowth.

PORTISHEAD (FIRST STATION)

A general view of the main building and station forecourt early in the twentieth century. A horse drawn carriage waits for passengers.

Looking north-east towards the site of the first station taken from the corner of Beach Road East and Station Road on 5th May 2010. The southern part of the station site, taken over by the Portishead B Power Station in 1955, is now occupied by Portishead Primary School.

PORTISHEAD (SECOND STATION)

A bleak view in 1954 of the front and forecourt of the station which served the town for 10 years until its closure in 1964.

The site, now occupied by a new petrol filling station associated with the nearby Waitrose store, on 25th September 2010. An earlier filling station, 'Station Garage', had incorporated much of the main structure of the 1954 station building.

PORTISHEAD (WCPLR)

Looking south-east at the 1907 station, the northern terminus of the Weston, Clevedon and Portishead Light Railway.

A view on 25th September 2010 of the station site at the north-west end of Wyndham Way. The rear of the White Lion public house is to the right. The line towards Clevedon followed the approximate line of Wyndham Way before turning south. The distant ridge of hills in the early photo can be seen on the left of this photograph.

PUXTON AND WORLE

Looking towards Bristol from the level crossing at St Georges. The main building (right) is on the down (towards Taunton) side with the station master's house beyond.

Apart from small sections of railings and gates, the station master's house seen in the earlier photograph is the principal survivor of the station buildings. As 'Station House', it continues in residential use on Station Road on 30th September 2010. West of the St Georges level crossing the signal box also remains.

RADSTOCK NORTH

The main building stands behind the up (towards Bath) platform, a striking feature being the large upward sloping canopy. In the far distance beyond the open footbridge is the goods yard. To the left is Radstock Market House.

From a similar viewpoint on 29th August 2010 landscaping and seating cover the west end of the former station site. The Market House is still there (left). Off the picture to the right car parking covers much of the station site whilst the goods yard has been redeveloped for housing.

RADSTOCK WEST

BELOW LEFT Looking east from the level crossing at the main building on the former up (towards Bristol) platform and the wooden shelter on the down. Behind the main building (right) is a terrace of houses along the south side of Fortescue Road.

BELOW RIGHT From the same viewpoint on 29th August 2010. The up side of the station has been redeveloped for shop units on the north side of Fortescue Road. The west end of these units can be seen behind the short lamppost in the centre of this photo. The terrace on the south side of the road seen in the earlier photo is still there (right). On the left of the photo is a derelict area in which the former down platform is buried beneath undergrowth in a proposed redevelopment site.

ROADWATER

A view looking north of the derelict station on the West Somerset Mineral Railway, a condition that lasted for some years. This illustration was published in the Railway Magazine in October 1934.

A complete transformation in this photo of 12th August 2010. The former platform and station building, with an extension, is now an attractive bungalow in the village of Roadwater.

ABOVE A train is entering from the south. Beyond the station building is the large goods shed.

LEFT From the same viewpoint the restored station building and platform in the recently opened retirement village, 'Sandford Station', on 20th May 2010. Note the renovated barge boards and cruciform style ridge tiles.

BELOW LEFT A close up of the Pullman Restaurant, the former goods shed, on 27th November 2010. Inside the building the signs are in a GWR style and colour. The large welcoming sign to Darlisette House refers to a set of new housing units.

BELOW The restored station master's house on the same day. Note the renovated barge boards.

SHAPWICK

A train en route from Highbridge to Glastonbury in 1963. To the right is the South Drain, one of many artificial water courses on the Somerset Levels.

The completely different scene on 19th July 2010. The station site is covered in vegetation and the trackbed is used as a pedestrian trail. The South Drain is much the same as in 1963.

SHEPTON MALLET HIGH STREET

Looking west from the A371 bridge in the 1930s, showing the main building (right), the two platforms and the covered footbridge. The top of the goods shed can just be glimpsed beyond the main building and footbridge.

From the same viewpoint the scene is much changed on 1st July 2010. The main station building has gone, its site being indicated by the white rectangular area in the bottom right of the picture. Between the two structures the goods shed office can be seen with a tall modern building to the left. Beyond these buildings the basic structure of the goods shed survives.

SOMERTON

A general view of the station looking north-east towards the high road bridge at the west end of West Street in the centre of the town. The main building incorporating the station offices is to the left.

All lineside trace of the station has gone on 27th August 2010 in this view south-west from the road bridge seen in the earlier picture. Some limited sections of railway related gates, posts and railings survive in the vicinity of the bridge and alongside Station Path that leads down to the station site behind the bushes to the left.

SPARKFORD

Looking north from the original A303 road bridge on 1st October 1966. Stone buildings serve passengers on both platforms with a large goods shed on the up (towards Castle Cary) side. In the bottom left of the photo is a cast iron gent's urinal.

It is hard to believe that this is the same view some 44 years later on 24th July 2010 with woodland and vegetation covering the former station site. In the far distance a concrete bridge carries the A303 Sparkford By-pass over the line, singled in May 1968.

TOP A view towards Bishops Lydeard on 30th October 1965 along the then wooden platform on which stands an early GWR wooden shelter. On the extreme left is the wall of the large goods shed and beyond this the ground level main building and cattle dock.

BOTTOM The now West Somerset Railway station from the same viewpoint some 45 years later on 5th August 2010. The platform now has a tarmac surface with paving slab edges, a new shelter replacing the early GWR structure is nearing completion. To the left a picnic area is on the site of the goods shed. The station building is in good condition following renovation.

STOGUMBER (2)

TOP Looking north on 30th October 1965 at the ground level station building with the large goods shed beyond (right). To the left the early GWR wooden shelter is at the south end of the wooden down platform.

BOTTOM From a similar viewpoint 45 years later on 5th August 2010. The renovated main building is to the right beyond which is the picnic area on the site of the goods shed. The new wooden shelter stands on the reconstructed platform which is supported by concrete blocks. In the far distance a 1992 shelter is at the north end of the platform.

TOP A view of the station from the east in about 1905 showing the 1868 overall roof covering the then three through tracks, two alongside the platform faces.

CENTRE The island platform looking down towards Exeter following the reconstruction of the station in the early 1930s. There are now 4 through tracks running alongside the platform faces. The island platform was unused from 1967 to 2000.

BOTTOM A view from about the same viewpoint on 22nd June 2010. Use of the island platform had been restored some 10 years earlier, a shelter and lift also being installed.

TOP The exterior and forecourt on the down (towards Exeter) side in about 1905. The two storey building is a survivor from the original 1842 station which only had buildings on this, the town side.

BOTTOM A similar view 105 years later on 22nd June 2010, modern cars replacing the horsedrawn carriages and early car. The 1842 building continues in use.

On 13th June 1964, the up (towards Bristol) building following the major reconstruction of the station in the early 1930s. The style is typical of that adopted by the GWR in that era.

The new booking office on 22nd June 2010 which came into use in March 1983 masking the exterior of the 1930s structure.

TEMPLECOMBE UPPER

TOP Looking east through the station prior to the extensive re-modelling in the 1930s. Note the fine glazed canopies.

CENTRE Again looking east at the post 1938 station, to the left is the new art-deco signal box, a replacement for the one on the left in the top photograph. The replacement canopies are of a typical Southern Railway style of that era.

BOTTOM The scene has changed again on 8th July 2010, some 28 years after the station reopened. A train to London (Waterloo) stands beside the 1990 shelter which replaced the 1930s building demolished in 1968. The 1938 signal box remains. The footbridge is an 1893 structure transferred from Buxted in Sussex.

ABOVE Looking east from a pedestrian footbridge in about 1912. A steam rail-motor is at the up (towards Bath) platform. This extends onto the bridge which takes the tracks over the road into Twerton where it forks from the Lower Bristol Road.

LEFT The three storey station building in use in about 1912, 5 years before its closure. The station nameboard is on the platform which stretches east onto the bridge which carries the line over the road into Twerton (left). Note the lateral extension to the bridge supporting the up platform.

LEFT The disused station building on 26th May 2010. When later seen in March 2011 the tall section of the building was surrounded by scaffolding.

Looking east in September 1966, the platform sited in a cutting. The photographer is standing on the Somerset/Devon border. The building above the signal box (right) incorporates the station offices and the station master's house.

The road frontage of the surviving building in residential use on 12th August 2010, the former station master's house, 'Station House', closest to the camera and beyond this, the former station offices, now 'The Booking Office'.

The inaccurate name on the gate of the access path leading to the converted goods shed, now a fine residence west of the station just over the border into Devon.

WASHFORD

LEFT A view towards Minehead in 1947 with, to the right, the goods shed in the goods yard. To the left is the small signal box which has been restored and fitted out in the manner of the Midford box on the Somerset and Dorset line. This work was undertaken by the Somerset & Dorset Railway Trust which is based at the station on the restored West Somerset Railway.

ABOVE Again looking west over 60 years later on 5th August 2010. Both the station building and the goods yard, now on the West Somerset Railway, have been restored to reflect the features of the Somerset & Dorset Railway. A large new building erected by the Somerset & Dorset Railway Trust, seen over the goods trucks, is used as a restoration workshop.

LEFT The rear of the main station building behind the down (towards Minehead) platform in the British Railways era in 1966. The nameboard is on the rear of the small signal box.

LEFT Little has changed 45 years later on 5th August 2010. The BR (British Railways) in the earlier photo has, however, been replaced by SDRT (Somerset & Dorset Railway Trust) and WSR (West Somerset Railway). The main building is now the museum of the Trust, containing many artefacts from stations on that famous railway.

TOP A Taunton bound train from Minehead enters the station in about 1961. The large goods shed can be seen behind the engine. The GWR pagoda style hut provides extra shelter for passengers on the single platform.

BOTTO From a similar viewpoint on 5th August 2010 as the West Somerset Railway's 1258 hrs train to Bishops Lydeard enters. The goods shed to the right of the engine is now the Watchet Boat Museum. The pagoda hut, for some years unused, is in use as a visitor centre and waiting room.

The terminus building of the original West Somerset Railway from Norton Junction to Watchet opened in 1862. This role explains its siting at right angles to the line, as seen on 30th October 1965.

The 1862 building now on the restored West Somerset Railway from Bishops Lydeard to Minehead in use as a booking office and shop. On 5th August 2010 the footbridge is closed with the notice 'Warning, dangerous structure'. Owned by West Somerset District Council, the bridge was removed in January 2011 for refurbishment.

WATCHET (WSMR)

TOP Looking north in 1935 through the site of the northern terminus of the West Somerset Mineral Railway which carried passengers from 1865 to 1898 and again in a limited way from 1907 to 1910. About 25 years after the station finally closed to passengers the main elements can still be seen: the stone goods shed (left), a wooden goods shed (middle) and the tall station house (middle right). Towards the camera, in front of the station house, the former platform is grass covered.

CENTRE Some 75 years later on 5th August 2010 the main elements of the station can still be identified with the stone goods shed (now a workshop) to the left, the wooden goods shed in the centre (now Spice House Restaurant) and the tall station house to the right.

LEFT Looking south into the station site with Station House, now in two flats with one for sale on 5th August 2010. The plaque above the small window states 'Old Station House 1855'.

Looking south from the road bridge on 7th June 1921. At that time only 2 tracks ran through the station. The goods shed on the left edge of the photo survives today. In 1931/2 the station was rebuilt with 4 through tracks.

Looking south from the same viewpoint as the 1921 photo, on 6th August 2010, again only 2 tracks. The goods shed survives to the left within the Swallowfield development. A section of the down platform can still be seen (centre left).

BELOW The forecourt on 9th May 1970, almost exactly 6 years after the station closed to passengers. The right hand photograph was taken from about the same viewpoint 40 years later on 6th August 2010, showing the station site now covered by the Swallowfield development.

WELLOW

ABOVE A train runs into the down (towards Radstock) platform at this attractive small station on the Somerset & Dorset Railway. Staff stand on both platforms, two holding milk churns, a familiar feature in rural areas. The main building on the up platform survives today (see below) but the shelter on the down side has gone.

LEFT A view on 29th August 2010 from the road to a public car park now occupying the site of the former small goods yard. The station building is now a fine house with the canopy still in place and extensions at both ends. A weather vane in the form of an engine and tender is on top of one chimney.

BELOW AND BELOW RIGHT Wellow signal box with No 47506 running past on 29th May 1965. Over 45 years later on 20th January 2011 the box survives as a part of a dwelling linked to a low modern structure. Access to the house is via Railway Lane.

WELLS PRIORY ROAD

ABOVE Looking south-east at the wooden train shed in 1934. Through the train shed are level crossing gates where the line continues across Priory Road to the former site of Wells East Somerset station. To the left, behind the parked carriage, is the station master's house, demolished in 1995 when the roundabout was constructed at the junction of Priory Road and the Wells Relief Road.

ABOVE AND LEFT The scene is almost unrecognisable over 75 years later on 20th May 2010. The road, Strawberry Way, follows the alignment of the former trackbed of the Wells- Cheddar-Yatton line (the Strawberry Line). The station site has been redeveloped including the large building for the builders' merchants, Travis Perkins. In the distance the roundabout is approximately on the site of the former level crossing. A stone plinth (left) indicating the site of the station is on the grass verge close to the foot of traffic lights. This is one of three plinths marking the sites of the three Wells stations.

WELLS TUCKER STREET

ABOVE Looking north through the station site on 16th April 1965, some 9 months after its closure. The line was still in use by freight trains mostly carrying stone, this continued until April 1969. The goods shed is beyond the station building and road bridge.

As with the Priory Road site, the scene taken from about the same viewpoint on 20th May 2010 is almost unrecognisable. The road is Strawberry Way, following the former trackbed of the line to Cheddar affectionately known as the Strawberry Line. The traffic lights in the centre of the photo are at the site of the former road bridge. Alongside the low roadside hedge to the right is a plinth marking the former site of the station.

The former Wells Tucker Street goods shed, the only significant former railway structure that survives from the three Wells stations. It is currently occupied by Roman Glass, Pine Plus and the Westfield Veterinary Centre.

WESTON (BATH)

LEFT Two staff pose in this early photograph of the attractive station on the north side of the Mangotsfield to Bath line. Note the barge boards and cruciform style ridge tiles.

BELOW LEFT The forecourt side of the building on 2nd March 2011, principally used by the radio station Bath Fm. Note the renovated fine barge boards. The ridge tiles seen in the earlier photo have gone.

BELOW The station master's house at the west end of Ashley Avenue which runs east from Station Road to the station building. Two metal posts, part of a former level crossing across Station Road, are just off the right of the photo. The large tree has grown on the north side of the former trackbed.

WESTON MILTON

A view east in 1963 of the two concrete platforms with shelters some 9 years before the Weston-super-Mare loop line was singled and the down platform closed.

From the same viewpoint some 47 years later on 30th September 2010. The down side platform has gone with loop line now a single track, it was transferred to the new Lympstone Commando station on the Exmouth branch in Devon.

WESTON-SUPER-MARE (FIRST STATION)

TOP An alas poor quality copy of a painting looking west at the first station opened in 1841 at the end of the single track Weston-super-Mare spur line.

BOTTOM A view on 28th September 2010 of the former station site at the end of Alexandra Parade now occupied by gardens, floral clock and a replica engine erected in 2006 to celebrate the 200th anniversary of Brunel's birth.

Looking west at the building then in use as a goods depot after withdrawal of passenger services in 1884. To the left is the clock tower of the Town Hall and on the extreme left another goods shed.

A view in a similar direction on 28th September 2010 showing the south end of the Tesco supermarket with the Hildesheim residential complex Note the clock tower of the Town Hall can just be seen above the tree on the extreme left.

The 1866 building looking north-east from an entrance on the east side of the northern section of Walliscote Road.

From a similar viewpoint on 28th September 2010. Retail units and a section of the Odeon Cinema (left) now forming the eastern frontage of Walliscote Road.

WESTON-SUPER-MARE (THIRD STATION)

Looking north east through the 1884 station. Note the fine glazed canopies and large covered footbridge.

From a similar viewpoint on the up platform on 28th September 2010. Basically little has changed but a detailed look shows the different form of the canopies extensively refurbished in 1992. The protective screen on the down platform (right) at the end of the canopy has gone and that on the up platform has been replaced. Modern lampposts have replaced the earlier more attractive versions.

Looking west at the down side of the 1884 station in the 1950s. Note the fine covered footbridge with tall structures at either end incorporating lift shafts.

Very little has changed 60 years later on 28th September 2010. The 0929 hrs train to Paignton, an EWS locomotive (on loan to First Great Western) stands at the down platform.

ABOVE The southern terminus of the Weston, Clevedon and Portishead Light Railway looking east. The main wooden building (left) is seen behind the buffers, the raised elevated wooden platform with shelter is centre right.

LEFT Looking east at the station site on 30th September 2010, a car stands where the west end of the platform stood. The former station building off to the left of the photo has gone. The large house is prominent in both photos.

BELOW LEFT The house occupied by the Traffic Manger of the Weston, Clevedon and Portishead Light Railway in 1898. Behind the fence is the southern terminus of the railway, the station building is a little way behind what appears to be a railway carriage.

BELOW A view of the building on 30th September 2010 at the corner of Milton Road and Ashcombe Road occupied by a Lloyd's pharmacy.

WESTON-SUPER-MARE LOCKING ROAD

Passengers leaving a train arrived at the excursion station in about 1924. Above the lamppost (left) the buildings aligning Locking Road run east. To the left above the engine tender is a railway related building on Locking Road.

The scene had changed so greatly that on 28th September 2010 it was difficult to take a photo to illustrate the changes. In the middle far distance and to the left is Locking Road. Much of the scene in the earlier photo is now covered by the road entrance to the Tesco car park (middle) and the extensive car park itself (right).

Looking west through the station on 29th August 1964. The main station building is on the up (south) platform and to its left is the station master's house. To the right is the goods shed. All these buildings survive today used by a transport firm

A view on 19th July 2010 at the former station site. To the left is the station master's house and in the centre is the station, both in residential use. Off the photo to the right is the former goods shed now in storage use.

WHITCHURCH HALT

Looking south from the A37 bridge at the 1925 halt with its GWR pagoda style hut.

Looking north in 1959 as the Class 4575 No 5542 hauls a train from Bristol to Radstock and Frome through the halt.

No trace of the halt remains but north of the surviving A37 bridge is a new housing development, a section of which covers the former trackbed. It includes a number of roads that remind local residents of the earlier railway era, including the appropriately named 'Halt End'.

A view towards Minehead in about 1912. The 1874 covered footbridge stands between the main building and goods shed on the down side (left) and beyond the up side shelter. To the left is the 1875 signal box. Note the water pump between the tracks.

Looking west again nearly 100 years later on 12th August 2010, the station now in use on the restored West Somerset Railway. From left to right on the down (towards Minehead) platform are a former store now in use as a shop and café, the restored main building, the renovated goods shed (the base of the Diesel and Electric Group) and the 1899 listed ex Swindon arc roofed metal building, now the West Somerset Railway locomotive maintenance and overhaul depot. There is no footbridge but on that date the ex Trowbridge footbridge was away from the site being restored before erection on the site of the 1874 footbridge. It was erected on 16 March 2011.

WILLITON (2)

TOP Looking east on 30th October 1965, a 1920 open lattice footbridge has replaced the earlier 1874 structure, now being sited between the main building and signal box on the down platform and east of the up side shelter.

CENTRE A very similar view 45 years later on 12th August 2010. The site for the erection of the ex Trowbridge footbridge is close to the Williton nameboard on the down platform (right), this occurred on 16 March 2011.

LEFT An exterior view of Williton station on the West Somerset Railway on 12th August 2010.

Class 2MT 2-6-2T No 41296 is standing at the down platform with the 1420 hrs Highbridge to Templecombe train on 19th April 1965. This platform is much shorter than that on the up side.

Everything has changed 45 years later on 8th July 2010, a housing estate has been developed over the former site of the station and goods yard.

Close to the housing is a road nameboard 'Pines Close', a reminder of the earlier era when the Pines Express en route from Manchester to Bournemouth passed through Wincanton station.

WINSCOMBE

TOP Looking south on 25th August 1958 as No 5569 hauls a train north towards Congresbury and Yatton. Note the fine horizontal canopy on the 1905 building which replaced the previous 1869 wooden structure.

CENTRE From a similar viewpoint on 9th December 2010. Behind the plinth the foundations of the station building can be seen, a feature of the year 2000 'Old Station Millennium Green'. The platform edge is to the right alongside which the Strawberry Line trail runs along the former trackbed.

LEFT The noticeboard at the entrance to the Old Station Millennium Green on 9th December 2010. It includes photos of the 1869 wooden station building.

WIVELISCOMBE

ABOVE The former up (towards Taunton) platform on 4th June 1966. An open alcove is between the two pavilion style arms of the building at right angles to the platform. Note the bay window of the former booking office. Beyond the platform is the goods shed.

LEFT The station building on 12th August 2010, the open waiting alcove has been filled in. The bay window survives as does a section of the paved platform surface. The building is occupied by the offices of a construction firm. The goods shed survives (far right) in industrial/storage use.

BELOW LEFT The rear of the station building on 18th July 1961, looking south-west.

BELOW In the opposite direction, the rear of the building nearly 50 years later on 12th August 2010.

WOOKEY

Looking west on 7th September 1963 from the bridge carrying the road to Wookey Hole over the Cheddar to Wells line. The goods shed is very large compared with the station building. The train is en route to Wells Tucker Street.

From the same viewpoint on 20th May 2010. The station itself has gone but the former goods shed and goods office are occupied by a car body shop (Wells Garage).

Staff and passengers pose in this view looking east at the small brick station similar in design to those at Langford and Blagdon on the Wrington Vale Light Railway which closed to passengers in 1931.

The station site on 8th March 2011, to the left is Wrington Veterinary Centre on the corner of Station Road and The Glebe. Behind the vehicles on the right is the entrance to 'Old Station Close' in which one of the houses is named 'The Sidings'.

YATTON

A Cheddar Valley train stands at the down bay platform in the 1930s. To the left the early large wooden canopy protects passengers both on the up (towards Bristol) main platform and the Clevedon branch platform (off left). An arc roof canopy serves passengers on the down platform, note the tall water tower.

From the same viewpoint over 70 years later on 28th September 2010 as the 1115 hrs Cross Country train from Bristol Temple Meads to Paignton speeds past the down platform. On the up platform the ex Dauntsey arc shaped canopy replaced the earlier version in 1956. To right and left car parking covers the land originally occupied by the Cheddar Valley and Clevedon lines. The footbridge has lost its roof but the original 1841 station buildings survive, now listed. When visited in September 2010 the down side building was being renovated for use as a community café at the north end of the Strawberry Line trail that follows the former trackbed of the Cheddar Valley line. The café opened on 13th December 2010.

TOP The 1853 station, now well buttressed in the 1964 photo. Following its closure as a passenger station in 1861, the building had various uses including the stabling of horses and as a goods depot, the latter ceasing in 1967. Just visible in the far distance to the right is the road bridge carrying the A30 Hendford Hill over the line towards Yeovil Town station.

BOTTOM The station site on 24th July 2010, the walkway, now created on the former trackbed, runs under the surviving A30 road bridge. To the left is the south wall of the Allied Carpets store.

YEOVIL HENDFORD HALT

TOP Looking east on 17th May 1962 just over 2 years before it closed. Through the bridge the roof of the former Yeovil Hendford station can just be seen to the left of the signals and engine.

BOTTOM The scene has completely changed by 24th July 2010. Lysander Road is to the right behind the trees. A former railway gate post survives just to the left of the no right turn sign in front of the MacDonalds building.

YEOVIL JUNCTION

ABOVE Looking across the south-west end of the station in about 1908/09 just after rebuilding associated with the introduction of a revised expanded track layout. The long covered footbridge serves two island platforms. The recently built station master's house, close to the footbridge steps, remains today as 'High Croft'.

LEFT The truncated footbridge looking north-east on 24th July 2010. It now only connects the approach road to the former up side island platform. The former down island platform is no longer served by trains, these calling only at the two faces of the up island.

BELOW Looking south-west along the up side island platform in the 1960s, the buildings dating from the 1907-1909 rebuild. Both island platforms are in use. To the right, in the distance, is the station master's house.

BELOW From a similar viewpoint on 24th July 2010. Trains no longer call at the former down island platform (left) though the surviving building without canopies is still in use. Beyond it is a recently constructed engine shed used by the South West Main Line Steam Company.

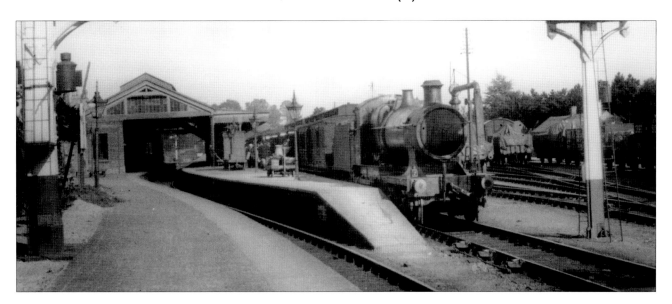

TOP Looking north-east in about 1925 showing the up (towards Castle Cary) single face platform, the island platform and the wooden train shed, removed in 1934. An unidentified Bulldog 4-4-0 stands with a train en route to Weymouth.

CENTRE Some 30 years later in the late 1950s a shuttle train from Yeovil Town station stands on the single track between the platforms. The train shed has gone, replaced by conventional platform canopies.

BOTTOM The station has hardly changed some 60 years later on 24th July 2010. Many railway historians are of the view that Yeovil Pen Mill very much retains the atmosphere of the GWR era.

A view north-east from the Sherborne Road bridge on 29th September 1963. A pannier tank engine hauling one carriage is at the outer face of the island platform. On the far right goods wagons stand on one of the many sidings.

In this view of 24th July 2010 the main change from the 1963 photo is the absence of goods activity, which ceased at Pen Mill in September 1965. The semaphore signals continue to control movements in the station area from the signal box seen beyond the far end of the island platform.

BELOW The road side frontage on 14th May 1972, a bus waits to carry passengers into the town centre. Nearly 40 years later on 24th July 2010 little has changed but the small entrance canopy has gone. A modern telephone box has replaced the earlier model and covered cycle stands have been provided.

YEOVIL TOWN (1)

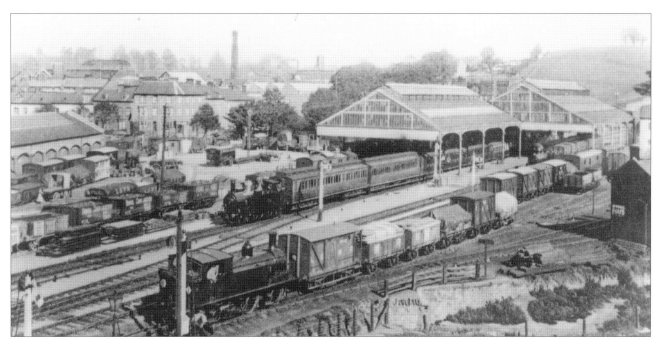

TOP Looking north over the station site in about 1910, two large glazed train sheds cover the platforms. There is much activity by both passenger and freight traffic.

CENTRE Some 50 years later on 30th July 1961 the large glazed train sheds have been replaced by conventional platform canopies in a Southern Railway style. A large goods shed is to the right.

BOTTOM About 50 years later on 24th July 2010 the station site is covered by large buildings occupied by retail and leisure uses. Note the prominent tree on the hill (right) that features at the centre of the 1961 photo and, less distinctly, in the top right of the 1910 view.

ABOVE The impressive road frontage on 18th May 1963, some 3 years before final closure.

LEFT From a similar viewpoint on 24th July 2010 the scene has completely changed. The only surviving relic of the station is the foundation stone relaid to the left of the tall lamppost in the centre of the photo, adjacent to Pizza Hut.

BELOW LEFT A close up of the 1860 foundation stone relaid in the heart of the retail and leisure complex. The wording above the date states, 'This is the foundation stone of Yeovil Town Station which stood on this site. The station was closed in 1967 and demolished in 1973'.

SOMERSET STATIONS & HALTS

SCHEDULE SHOWING GRID REFERENCE, OPENING AND CLOSING DATES AND RECENT/CURRENT (2010/2011) USE OF THE SITE.

ALFORD HALT   ST 606318
Opened: 21.7.1905 on the Castle Cary – Charlton Mackrell section of the GWR cut-off line, Castle Cary – Cogload Junction originally opened on 1.7.1905.
Closed: 10.9.1962 with the withdrawal of local passenger services Castle Cary – Taunton.
No lineside structures now remain. Railings alongside the footpath from the road to the site of the down platform are still there on the south side of the road over bridge.

ASHCOTT   ST 450397
Opened: 7.1856 on the Highbridge Wharf – Glastonbury section of the Somerset Central Railway originally opened on 28.8.1854. *Station opened as Ashcott and Meare but renamed Ashcott in 1876.*
Closed: Passengers: 7.3.1966 with closure of the Evercreech Junction – Highbridge line to passenger traffic; Goods: 13.7.1964.
Following demolition of the original station agent's (master's) house due to subsidence, a former porter at Ashcott built a new bungalow just to the east. A small building adjacent to, and west of, the original house that contained the waiting room/booking office survives, used for storage. Remnants of the bases of the platform supports can be seen alongside the tarmac track that runs in front of the new bungalow. Two former level crossing gate posts remain on the east side of the road west of the former station site, an adjacent fence bears the sign 'The Old Station'.

ATHELNEY   ST 345286
Opened: Passengers: 1.10.1853 with the opening to passenger traffic of the Durston – Yeovil Hendford branch from the Bristol & Exeter Railway; Goods: 26.10.1853 with the opening of the branch to goods traffic.
Closed: Passengers: 15.6.1964 with closure of the Durston – Yeovil line; Goods: 6.7.1964.
No remains of the station buildings and platforms survive alongside the current line between Castle Cary and Taunton. The former down side (towards Taunton) 1908 main building is now in use as the sports pavilion for the nearby Stoke St Gregory playing fields. Purchased for £25, it was cut into

three sections and moved to its new site by farm tractors. When viewed in August 2010, it was resplendent, painted bright green. The signal box (1906), closed in April 1986, was dismantled 3 years later and re-erected at Staverton on the South Devon Railway. In the former goods yard on the down side a building formerly known as 'the Engine Room' (or 'House') survives as a private workshop for an adjacent house. Also surviving is a former goods platform on which a store now stands and evidence of the site of a former hand cranked crane and a weighbridge base. Close to the west of the site, and south of the now automatic level crossing, is the station master's house in residential use 'Old Station House'.

AVON RIVERSIDE   ST 682687
Opened: 25.4.2004 with the opening of the southern extension of the restored Avon Valley Railway, Bitton - Avon Riverside.
Closed: Remains open for services on the Avon Valley Railway.
A single concrete platform with no shelter just south-east of the railway bridge over the River Avon and thus sited in Somerset.

AXBRIDGE   ST 432547
Opened: 3.8.1869 with the opening of the Yatton – Cheddar section of the Cheddar Valley & Yatton Railway.
Closed: Passengers: 9.9.1963 with closure of the Yatton – Witham line to passenger traffic; Goods: 10.6.1963.
The re-aligned A371 runs along the former trackbed north of, and in front of, the platform side of the former station. The station building itself, including the barge boards, survives in good condition, in use today as the Axbridge Youth Centre. To the east of the station building, the goods shed, including the canopy and barge boards, also survives, in industrial use. The station master's house continues in residential use on the north side of the road, opposite the goods shed.

BASON BRIDGE   ST 346459
Opened: 7.1856 on the Highbridge Wharf – Glastonbury section of the Somerset Central Railway originally opened on 28.8.1854.

Closed: Passengers: 7.3.1966 with closure of the Evercreech Junction – Highbridge line to passenger traffic.
Following closure in 1966, the station building was demolished in November 1968. Milk trains generated by the large milk production factory east of the station continued through the station site until 2nd October 1972. Construction of the M5 motorway some 1½ miles to the west of the station severed the line and all rail traffic through Bason Bridge ceased. The platform survives largely hidden beneath brambles and undergrowth but in July 2010 a small section of the platform and east end ramp could be seen. The station master's house west of the station survives in residential use at the end of a private drive.

BATH GREEN PARK   ST 746648

Opened: 4.8.1869 as the terminus of the Mangotsfield (Glos) – Bath branch from the Bristol – Gloucester line. *It was only in 1951 that the suffix 'Green Park' was added officially, prior to this the name 'Queen Square' had been used unofficially.*
Closed: Passengers: 7.3.1966 with the withdrawal of passenger services on the Bath – Poole line; Goods: 31.5.1971.
Following closure to passengers in 1966, the station buildings deteriorated due to vandalism, damage and decay. In November 1971 the main building was designated as a Grade II listed structure and a year later the City Council purchased the site and undertook a number of urgent repairs. There had been spasmodic use of the site as a car park but otherwise there was little use. A number of schemes were proposed including one that involved the demolition of the fine train shed. In October 1979 a scheme was agreed between the City Council, British Railways Board and Sainsbury's for the restoration of the station building and the construction of a large supermarket. The renovated building was formally opened by HRH Princess Margaret on 1st December 1982.

Today the Sainsbury's supermarket and Homebase occupy most of the Green Park Station site with the latter on the former goods yard and engine shed site west of the River Avon. The main building is well used with the booking hall occupied by the Green Park Brasserie. Many of the former station offices and rooms survive in their original form, used by retail outlets and offices.. A number of stalls occupy the former departure (south side) platform. Half of the renovated glazed train shed covers car parking with the remainder boarded over used for events and exhibitions. The vaults beneath the departure platform are occupied by 'South Vaults', an ethical centre bringing together charities, community and campaign groups under one roof. These include the Volunteer Centre for Bath and North East Somerset, the Shaw Trust and the CTC Cycle Organisation.

BATH SPA   ST 753643

Opened: 31.8.1840 as the terminus of the Bristol – Bath section of the GWR Bristol – London line. The line on to London opened 30.6.1841 through Box Tunnel.

Closed: Passengers: remains open for services on the Bristol – London and Bristol – Southampton/Weymouth line; Goods: 5.1967 (Depot), 31.12.1980 (full load traffic).

In 2010 the basic features of the 1840s station remain apart from the early overall train shed dismantled in 1897. In that year an up-bay platform was added but was taken out of use in 1967. Also now lost is the unusual open girder footbridge which, from 1845 to 1936, linked directly from the east end of the up (towards London) platform across the road into the Royal Hotel. In 1962 the entrance and exit facilities on the down (Widcombe) side were closed and the pedestrian subway renewed. In 1965/66 the 1890s hydraulic lifts, one for passengers and one for luggage for each platform were removed. In late 2010 work commenced on the provision of new lifts. Today the station, Grade II listed, is in good condition with many of the original features restored. The up-side refreshment room continues in use, being renovated in late 2010, and the up and down platform waiting rooms also survive. The elevated signal box above the canopy of the down platform has gone, removed after its closure on 25th January 1968.

BATHAMPTON   ST 778666

Opened: 2.2.1857 as a junction station on the GWR main line with the opening of the Bathampton – Bradford Junction branch of the Wilts, Somerset & Weymouth Railway.
Closed: Passengers: 3.10.1966; Goods: 10.6.1963.
The buildings and platforms were demolished partly associated with the re-modelling of trackwork at Bathampton Junction, just east of the station that allows faster passage of trains leaving the main London line towards Westbury and the south coast. No trace remains of the station at trackside. The only remains are the station entrance gateposts, the gate and an adjoining kissing gate at the head of the station approach road, alongside which stands the station master's house, continuing in residential use, 'Station House'.

BATHFORD HALT   ST 787671

Opened: 18.3.1929 on the Bath – Chippenham section of the GWR Bristol – London line originally opened on 30.6.1841.
Closed: 4.1.1965.
There are no trackside remains but there is evidence of the two access footpaths leading to the halt on the embankment just to the east of the impressive stone bridge carrying the main London line over the A363. On the down (south) side the alignment of the former footpath is now a tarmac track providing access to the tracks for maintenance. On the up-side a low wall of breeze blocks fills a gap in the stone wall where the path left the pavement.

BAWDRIP HALT   ST 343398

Opened: 7.7.1923 on the Bridgwater branch of the Somerset & Dorset Railway opened on 21.7.1890
Closed: 1.12.1952, with closure of the Bridgwater line to passenger traffic.
No trace of the halt survives but the village hall just behind the station site is still there. A section of the former

trackbed west of the halt now forms the garden of a modern bungalow, whimsically called 'Essandee'. A stone wall that supported the trackbed and a stone rail over-bridge west of the former halt remain today.

BEAM BRIDGE   ST 110195

Opened: 1.5.1843 as a temporary southern terminus of the Bristol & Exeter Railway as it extended beyond Taunton.
Closed: 1.5.1844 with the opening of the next section of the Bristol & Exeter Railway on to Exeter.
No trace of this very short-lived station survives today.

BINEGAR   ST 616492

Opened: 20.7.1874 with the opening of the Bath Extension of the Somerset & Dorset Railway, Evercreech Junction – Bath.
Closed: Passengers 7.3.1966 with the withdrawal of passenger services on the Bath – Poole line; Goods: 10.6.1963.
The station building and platforms have gone, the site being largely occupied by a large new house appropriately called 'The Beechings'. The semi-detached station master's (or agent's) and signalman's houses are in residential use as is the converted large goods shed. A gate and an old kissing gate remain close to the surviving houses. A new house 'The Halt' stands on the former embankment at the north-east end of the station site close to the former rail over bridge whose abutments remain beside Station Road.

BISHOPS LYDEARD   ST 164290

Opened : 31.3.1862 with the opening of the West Somerset Railway, Norton Junction – Watchet.
Closed: Passengers: 4.1.1971 with closure of the Minehead branch, Norton Junction – Minehead.
Reopened: 9.6.1979 with the opening of the Bishops Lydeard – Stogumber section of the restored West Somerset Railway. Following its reopening in mid 1979, the station has undergone extensive renovation and development in the style of a GWR branch line facility. The original main building on the down (west) platform has been restored and is now the headquarters of the West Somerset Railway Association. South of the building, the goods shed, with an extension at its southern end, is now the Gauge Museum housing a display of rolling stock, other railway items and a signal cabin. Upstairs is a large model railway and downstairs a film and lecture theatre. Between the WSRA headquarters and the goods shed is a 1977 structure erected and used by the Taunton Model Railway Group.

There have been a number of recent changes on the up (towards Taunton) platform which was extended in 1996 at the south end beyond the signal box in order to accommodate an 11 carriage train. The original small waiting room is now the 'Book Case', used for book sales and other information pamphlets. Alongside to the south is the West Somerset Association shop and buffet (The Wheeltappers) opened in 1996. Attached to its southern end is the 2004 ticket office; this replaced a small 1992 structure at the

up side station entrance which still stands. The impressive 1906 signal box at the south end of the up platform, decommissioned and gutted in 1970, has been completely restored for full use. The platform lampposts are of GWR origin, transferred from the closed Tiverton Junction station. The large water tank beyond the south end of the station originated at a large nursery near Ilminster.

The considerable car parking problem, associated with its role as the southern terminus of the West Somerset Railway, was tackled in 1997 with the development of a car park and toilet block behind the up platform. The car park added to the earlier facility on the former up-side goods yard. The station master's house, behind the south end of the down platform, is used as holiday accommodation; the two porters' cottages behind the north end of the platform continue in residential use. Finally over the years the station gardens have received many awards in the 'Taunton in Bloom' competition. These add to the awards for the operation of the restored station itself.

BLAGDON   ST 503597

Opened: 4.12.1901 as the terminus of the Wrington Vale Light Railway, Congresbury – Blagdon.
Closed: Passengers: 14.9.1931 with closure of the Wrington Vale Light Railway to passenger traffic; Goods: 1.11.1950 with closure of the Wrington – Blagdon section of the line to goods traffic.
The former station building and platform are preserved in a residential development, a large modern two storey house having been built in the 1960s behind and linked to the 1901 structure. The house was constructed using in part stone from the demolished Worle station. The former trackbed is laid out as a lawn. Two old station lampposts are alongside the road entrance, one with 'Blagdon' on the lamp glass and the other with a notice 'To GWR Station'. The overall development on Station Road is called 'Little Halt'.

BLEADON AND UPHILL   ST 326577

Opened: 11.1871 on the Bristol – Bridgwater section of the Bristol & Exeter Railway originally opened on 14.6.1841.
Opened as Uphill but renamed one year later.
Closed: 5.10.1964.
For some years after closure in 1964 a small railway museum operated on the up-side (towards Bristol) section of the site, the station buildings being retained. The museum closed during the 1980s, the buildings were demolished in the early 1990s and today the site is laid out as a garden. The station master's house, a little way behind the up platform, continues, with extensions, in residential use.

BLUE ANCHOR   ST 022435

Opened: 16.7.1874 with the opening of the Minehead Railway, Watchet – Minehead. *Early names of the station were Blue Anchor Excursion Platform and Bradley Gate.*
Closed: Passengers: 4.1.1971 with closure of the Minehead branch, Norton Junction – Minehead: Goods: 19.8.1963.
Reopened: 28.3.1976 with the opening of the Minehead –

Blue Anchor section of the restored West Somerset Railway. Since its reopening on the West Somerset Railway in 1976 extensive renovation has been undertaken on the up (north side) platform. The main station building with the booking office and waiting room has been restored using GWR fittings, many of them from the station itself but also including a cast iron barrier rescued from the station at Somerton. A 1989 shelter, between the main building and the surviving 1904 ladies room, replaced an original structure demolished because of its dangerous condition. The down side waiting room has also been restored and since 1985 has housed a small GWR museum run by the West Somerset Steam Railway Trust, opened to celebrate the 150th anniversary of the GWR.

The 1904 signal box, with its original 17 lever frame, at the west end of the platform continues in use, including the large wheel which controls the level crossing gates, the only surviving example in the South West. The station gardens are an attractive feature. As with other stations on the WSR Blue Anchor has been used for filming including transformation into Polgarwith in an Agatha Christie 'Poirot' story.

BREAN ROAD HALT   ST 324544

Opened 17.6.1929 on the Bristol – Bridgwater section of the Bristol – Exeter line originally opened on 14.6.1841. *Also described in some timetables as 'Brean Road for Brean Sands' or 'Lympsham Halt'.*
Closed: 2.5.1955.
Today there are no trackside remains of the halt closed 55 years ago. The access on the down (towards Taunton) side can be readily identified with old rail posts and a surviving iron gate at the head of the path at road side. One vertical rail on the Brean side of the road over bridge also indicates the original position of the access path on the up side.

BRENT KNOLL   ST 324514

Opened 1.11.1875 on the Bristol – Bridgwater section of the Bristol – Exeter line originally opened on 14.6.1841.
Closed: Passengers: 4.1.1971; Goods: 6.6.1963.
There are no trackside remains of this station. On the down side the cleared site of the buildings can readily be seen at the end of a long approach road alongside which a house is named 'Journeys End'. On the up (towards Bristol) side an industrial building, occupied by a high pressure cleaning operative, stands at the end of the former access road.

BRIDGWATER   ST 308369

Opened: 14.6.1841 as the terminus of the first section of the Bristol & Exeter Railway, Bristol – Bridgwater.
Closed: Passengers: remains open principally for local services on the Bristol – Taunton – Exeter line. Also limited through peak hour services to and from London (Paddington); Goods: 11.1965.
The principal buildings, listed Grade II, incorporating original Bristol & Exeter Railway features, are today in a reasonable condition. Recent refurbishment has included a renovated booking hall on the up (towards Bristol) platform,

an improved station frontage and a redeveloped forecourt including parking facilities. However, some wooden sections of the footbridge, platform canopies and platform screen are in a poor condition. 'Station House' and 'Station Cottages' remain in residential use but the Railway Hotel on the up side has been replaced by a modern development, Byron Wynn Autos.

BRIDGWATER NORTH (S&D)   ST 304374

Opened: 21.7.1890 as the terminus of the Bridgwater branch of the Somerset & Dorset Railway. *The suffix 'North' was only added in 1949, prior to this 'S & D' was used.*
Closed: Passengers: 1.12.1952 with closure of the branch to passenger traffic; Goods: 7.7.1962 (from October 1954 access via former GWR lines).
After closure to passengers much of the site was used for some years as a depot for British Road Services. The station building itself was demolished in August 1984, as was the engine shed, used as a store, in December 1985. The goods shed survived until it burnt down in July 1985. The station master's house, renovated in the mid 1980s, also burnt down three years later and was demolished when work began on the development of a Sainsbury's supermarket. This, with associated car parks, now covers much of the station site and goods yard and no structures survive. A plaque recording the former use of the site as a station is fixed to the supermarket wall close to the customer entrance. It was erected on 21st July 1990, exactly 100 years after the station opened.

BRISTOL ROAD HALT   ST 350623

Opened: 7.1912 on the Weston-super-Mare – Clevedon section of the Weston, Clevedon & Portishead Light Railway, opened on 1.12.1897
Closed: 20.5.1940 with closure of the line.
No trace of this halt, at which there was no platform or shelter, can now be seen.

BROADSTONE HALT   ST 387674

Opened: 7.1918 on the Weston-super Mare – Clevedon section of the Weston, Clevedon & Portishead Light Railway opened on 1.12.1897.
Closed: 20.5.1940 with closure of the line.
Today there is no trace of this halt which comprised a small sentry box type shelter but no platform. In May 2010 the local Weston, Clevedon & Portishead Railway Group recreated the wooden shelter and placed it in position to mark the 70th anniversary of the last day (18th May 1940) that a passenger train passed through the halt. This shelter is now at the Oakham Treasures Museum near Portbury.

BRUTON   ST 688348

Opened: 1.9.1856 with the opening of the Frome – Yeovil section of the Wilts, Somerset & Weymouth Railway.
Closed: Passengers: remains open for services on the Bristol – Weymouth line; Goods: 5.4.1965.
Downgraded to a halt in October 1969, the buildings were subsequently demolished. When visited in 2002 passengers

were served by two bus stop style shelters in poor condition. A revisit in July 2010 found much improved facilities with recent metal and glass shelters, new platform lamps and a modern metal footbridge. Limited sections of the old railings remain at the west end of the down platform. Local information is displayed provided by the 'Friends of Bruton Station', financed by First Great Western through the Community Rail Partnership for the Heart of Wessex Line. Attractive flower pots are sited on both platforms. A modern metal building stands on the site of the goods shed on the up (towards Castle Cary) side at the west end of the station, West End Garage.

BURNHAM-ON-SEA   ST 304488
Opened: 3.5.1858 with the opening of the Highbridge – Burnham-on-Sea extension of the Somerset Central Railway. *Suffix 'on Sea' added from 12.7.1920.*
Closed: Passengers: 29.10.1951 with the withdrawal of regular passenger services; 8.9.1962 with the withdrawal of excursion trains; Goods: 20.5.1963.
Today the former station site and trackbed has been taken over by the new road from the sea front to Highbridge (Marine Drive). The station building was demolished by 1967 but the long excursion platform on the south side survived for some years. The building, with its overall roof, was close to the current Queen Elizabeth II Jubilee water feature erected in 2002.

The tiny signal box, at the east end of the north side platform, closed in 1960. At first preserved at the Bleadon & Uphill museum and then at the Toddington base of the Gloucestershire Warwickshire Railway, it was finally restored and is now exhibited at the Washford site of the Somerset & Dorset Railway Trust. The nearby 'Somerset & Dorset' public house, with its appropriate engine sign, is nearby at the junction of High Street and Abingdon Street, the sole reminder of the earlier railway era at Burnham-on-Sea.

BURRINGTON   ST 483597
Opened: 4.12.1901 with the opening of the Wrington Vale Light Railway, Congresbury – Blagdon.
Closed: Passengers: 14.9.1931 with closure of the Wrington Vale Light Railway to passenger traffic; Goods: 1.11.1950 with closure of the Wrington – Blagdon section of the line to goods traffic.
The 1907 station building, which replaced the original small shelter, was demolished in 1958 some 27 years after it closed to passengers. Its cutting site was subsequently infilled. The former alignment of the line is now difficult to trace, though the location of a road over bridge north-west of the station can be identified by a shallow hump on Langford Lane close to its junction with the A358. The 1907 station master's house at this junction continues in residential use, with extensions, 'Station House'.

CADBURY ROAD HALT   ST 448742
Opened: 7.8.1907 with the opening of the Clevedon – Portishead section of the Weston, Clevedon & Portishead

Light Railway.
Closed: 20.5.1940 with closure of the line.
No trace of the halt, at which a waiting shelter was provided, can now be seen.

CAMERTON   ST 682579
Opened: Goods: 1.3.1882 with the opening of the Hallatrow – Camerton branch to goods traffic; Passengers: 1.4.1882 with the opening of the branch to passenger traffic.
Closed: Passengers 21.9.1925 with closure of the Cam Valley line, Hallatrow – Limpley Stoke to passenger traffic; Goods 15.2.1951 with complete closure of the Hallatrow – Limpley Stoke line.
Also temporary closure to passenger traffic, originally as a war time measure, 22.3.1915 – 9.7.1923.
Today virtually all trace of the railway era at Camerton has gone, demolition having occurred in the 1950s. The station site, identified on a display board at nearby Camerton Batch, was to the rear of two bungalows in Bridge Place Road close to its junction with Camerton Hill. A section of former railway railings can be seen in the valley to the rear of the bungalows. The former road over bridge west of the station site has gone. Some six years after it closed to passengers, the station was the location of filming for Arnold Ridley's 'The Ghost Train'.

CASTLE CARY   ST 635335
Opened: 1.9.1856 with the opening of the Frome – Yeovil section of the Wilts, Somerset & Weymouth Railway.
Closed: Passengers: remains open for services on the London Paddington – West Country and Bristol – Yeovil – Weymouth lines; Goods: 3.10.1966
By the late 1950s decline had set in, in particular with the withdrawal of stopping services between Westbury and Taunton. In 1985, in conjunction with alterations to trackwork and signalling, the down (towards Taunton) platform was rebuilt so that trains on the Yeovil – Weymouth line could call at either face. This gave the extra capacity needed to accommodate the reintroduction of stops at Castle Cary of West of England express trains en route to and from London (Paddington). (In the summer 2010 timetable there were 8 direct trains to and 9 from the capital calling at the station.)

A major event each year in late June is use of the station by music lovers at the Glastonbury Festival held at nearby Pilton. Special trains call at the station and on the Monday following the 2010 Festival it was reported that some 13,000 passengers used the station. (In early July the station was still adorned with posters erected for the benefit of Festival goers!)

Today the original main station building on the up (towards Westbury) platform remains in good condition but the 1856 down side shelter was lost in the 1984 rebuilding, replaced by a concrete hut. The 1954/55 goods shed, which replaced an earlier shed damaged in the Second World War, survives but, when seen in July 2010, appeared to be unused and becoming derelict. There was evidence of a previous use for car washing of vehicles left in the station car park which now covers the adjacent former goods yard. In 2007 Castle Cary station was given the accolade of 'Small Station of the Year' in the annual National Railway Awards, this being recorded on a plaque inside the main building's well appointed waiting room. The station master's house continues in residential use, 'Station House', a little distance from the station at the junction of the B3152 (Station Road) and A.371 (Ansford Hill).

CHARD CENTRAL   ST 329093

Opened: 11.9.1866 with the opening of the Taunton – Chard branch from the Bristol & Exeter Railway. *Opened as Chard Joint, renamed Chard 1.3.1928 and Chard Central 26.9.1949.*

Closed: Passengers: 10.9.1962 with closure of the Taunton – Chard Junction line to passenger traffic; Goods: 3.2.1964; Private siding closed 3.10.1966. Temporary closure to all traffic 3.2.1951 – 7.5.1951 due to fuel crisis.

Previous visits to the site indicated occupation of the station building, including the train shed, by a tyre depot (1994) and by an engine parts and international shipping firm (2002). Unfortunately the June 2010 visit showed that the building was unoccupied and in a desolate state. Enquiries were being invited for its future commercial use. The site is on Great Western Road and nearby to the south is housing in 'Old Station Court'.

CHARD JUNCTION   ST 340048

Opened: 19.7.1860 with the opening of the Yeovil Junction – Exeter section of the London & South Western Railway. *Opened as Chard Road, changed to Chard Junction August 1872, 9 years after branch line to Chard Town opened.*

Closed: Passengers: 7.3.1966; Goods: 18.4.1966.

Following closure of the station in 1966, the up (towards Crewkerne and Yeovil) side buildings and goods shed survived into the 1980s. In 2010 the principal remaining elements were a section of the up platform and the 1982 signal box at the Crewkerne end of this platform adjacent to the level crossing. The separate branch platform behind the main up platform across the former station forecourt also survives, now in a coal yard. An isolated buffer stands close to the large milk depot on the down side of the line, which ceased to be rail linked in 1980.

The former 'Chard Road Hotel' on the up side, east of the level crossing, now advertises en-suite accommodation in 'Three Counties' , a name reflecting its location close to the borders of Dorset, Devon and Somerset. To the north of the station site is 'Old Station House' on the west side of Station Road which links to Perry Street.

CHARD TOWN   ST 328087

Opened: 8.5.1863 with the opening of the Chard Road (later Junction) - Chard branch of the London & South Western Railway.

Closed: Passengers: 1.1.1917 when the GWR undertook to work the line between Chard Junction and Chard Joint

stations; Goods: 18.4.1966.

Following closure of the goods facilities that had continued at the site after passenger services ceased in 1917, the sidings were lifted in 1967. The whole site on Tapstone Road is now covered by road improvements and a petrol filling station linked to the adjacent Tesco store.

CHARLTON MACKRELL   ST 533289

Opened 1.7.1905 as a temporary terminus with the opening of the Castle Cary – Charlton Mackrell section of the GWR cut off line, Castle Cary – Cogload Junction.

Closed: Passengers and Goods: 10.9.1962 with the withdrawal of local passenger services between Castle Cary and Taunton.

Today Station Road, at the west end of the former station site, is the only direct reminder of the railway era. The down (south) part of the station site is now occupied by the Charltons Community Hall. The former station site on the up side, occupied in 2002 by the 'Old Quarry' retailing building and paving stones, was in August 2010 closed off by a padlocked gate. High Speed Trains pass through the site between Paddington and the West Country.

CHEDDAR   ST 453532

Opened: 3.8.1869 with the opening of the Yatton – Cheddar section of the Cheddar Valley & Yatton Railway.

Closed: Passengers: 9.9.1963 with closure of the Yatton – Witham line to passenger traffic; Goods: 29.11.1965; Private siding closed 28.3.1969.

The overall station roof was demolished in 1964, a year after the station closed to passengers. Much of the station site is today occupied by Wells Cathedral Stone Masons, a plaque dated 17th September 2004 records 20 years of such use. The offices are housed in the station building with the trackbed now covered by a large shed used for stone cutting. The adjacent goods shed has been converted into a fine house within modern housing on Old Station Close. The station master's house, with prominent gable barge boards, continues in residential use, 'Station House', on Wideatts Road.

CHILCOMPTON   ST 644515

Opened: 20.7.1874 with the opening of the Bath Extension of the Somerset & Dorset Railway, Evercreech Junction - Bath.

Closed: Passengers: 7.3.1966 with the withdrawal of passenger services on the Bath – Poole line; Goods: 15.6.1964.

After closure in 1966 much of the station site was used for storage by Sheppard's Saw Mills until this closed in the mid 1980s. Most of the station buildings were cleared in 1991. The cutting in which the line from Midsomer Norton entered the station site from the east has been filled in. Today a new road, Station Mead, is approximately on the alignment of the former station approach road; a house at the west end of the road is called 'Upline'. Beyond the west end of Station Mead the author found remnants of the former down platform in 2002 but this was not possible in August 2010 because of heavy undergrowth and extensive brambles. Much of the railway land beyond the west end of the station site is occupied by Massey Wilcox, a haulage firm.

CLAPTON ROAD HALT   ST 466752
Opened: 7.8.1907 with the opening of the Clevedon – Portishead section of the Weston, Clevedon & Portishead Light Railway
Closed: 20.5.1940 with closure of the line.
No trace of the halt, at which no shelter was provided, can now be seen.

CLEVEDON   ST 408711
Opened: 28.7.1847 with the opening of the Yatton – Clevedon branch of the Bristol & Exeter Railway.
Closed: Passengers: 3.10.1966 with closure of the branch; Goods: 10.6.1963
The buildings at Clevedon were demolished in May 1968 and the whole site of the station and goods yard was subsequently redeveloped as the Triangle Centre, today occupied principally by a Morrisons supermarket. The sole reminder of the previous railway presence is a war memorial erected by Clevedon Town Council commemorating the residents of the town who left by the GWR station and 'gave their lives in the defence of our freedom and liberty' A curved section of rail forms the rear of the memorial sited at the front of the shopping complex facing on to Station Road.

CLEVEDON (WCPLR)   ST 407710
Opened: 1.12.1897 with the opening of the Weston-super-Mare – Clevedon section of the Weston, Clevedon and Portishead Light Railway.
Closed: 20.5.1940 with closure of the line.
Today virtually all the former station site is covered by the Morrisons store car park at the Triangle Centre. However, the building that housed the ticket office at the south-east end of Lower Queens Road survives, occupied in mid 2010 by 'Jet Shoes Shoe Repairs'.

CLEVEDON ALL SAINTS HALT   ST 417717
Opened: 8.1917 on the Clevedon – Portishead section of the Weston, Clevedon & Portishead Light Railway originally opened on 7.8.1907
Closed: 20.5.1940 with closure of the line.
No trace of the halt, at which there was no platform or shelter, can now be seen.

CLEVEDON EAST HALT   ST 417714
Opened: 7.8.1907 with the opening of the Clevedon - Portishead section of the Weston, Clevedon & Portishead Light Railway.
Closed: 20.5.1940 with closure of the line.
No trace of this halt, at which a fairly large wooden shelter was provided, can now be seen.

CLUTTON   ST 627593
Opened: 3.9.1873 with the opening of the Bristol & North Somerset Railway, Bristol – Radstock.
Closed: Passengers: 2.11.1959 with closure of the Bristol – Radstock – Frome line to passenger traffic; Goods: 15.6.1964.
The station building and platform have gone, the only surviving structure on this once large station site is a small brick building in the former lower goods yard, the northern section of which is now a lorry depot. When visited in June 2010, the first phase of a housing development, appropriately called 'The Sidings', was nearing completion on the southern section of the yard; two further phases awaited planning clearance. The station master's house with an extension on its eastern side continues in residential use on Station Road. Further up the hill on the same road is the 'Railway Inn', a direct reminder of Clutton's railway era.

COLE   ST 671337
Opened: 3.2.1862 with the opening of the Cole – Templecombe section of the Dorset Central Railway and the Cole – Glastonbury section of the Somerset Central Railway.
Closed: Passengers: 7.3.1966 with closure of the Bath Green Park – Poole line to passenger traffic; Goods: 5.4.1965.
The up platform shelter was demolished in June 1967 but, after remaining empty for some years, the station building was converted into a house with a fine garden, 'The Old Station'. The adjacent station master's house continues in residential use, 'Station House'. During the 1990s housing was developed on the former goods yard south of the station; today the nearest house to the former station building is named 'The Pines' (a reference to the former Pines Express train from Manchester to Bournemouth that once passed through Cole). This housing is accessed by Old Station Lane. The nearby former Railway Hotel is in residential use, 'Hillside'.

COLEHOUSE LANE HALT   ST 399697
Opened: 1.12.1897 with the opening of the Weston-super-Mare – Clevedon section of the Weston, Clevedon & Portishead Light Railway.
Closed: 20.5.1940 with closure of the line.
Provided originally with a long narrow shelter but no platform, no remnants of this halt can now be seen.

COMBE HAY HALT   ST 730601
Opened: 9.5.1910 with the opening of the Cam Valley line, Camerton – Limpley Stoke.
Closed: 21.9.1925 with closure of the Hallatrow – Limpley Stoke line to passenger traffic. Also temporary closure, originally as a wartime measure, 22.3.1915 – 9.7.1923. Today, some 85 years after it closed, no trace of the halt can be seen. West of the site two sections of brick wall indicate the location of a former short tunnel.

COMBEROW   ST 030354
Opened: 4.9.1865 with passenger services on the West Somerset Mineral Railway, Comberow – Watchet.

Closed: 8.11.1898 with the withdrawal of passenger services on the line.
Also a temporary limited revival of passenger services 1907 – 1910.
In the mid 1930s the station building was demolished for re-use of the stone materials. Traces of the platform survive as does the nearby station master's house.

CONGRESBURY   ST 432639

Opened: 3.8.1869 with the opening of the Yatton – Cheddar section of the Cheddar Valley & Yatton Railway.
Closed: Passengers: 9.9.1963 with closure of the Yatton – Witham line to passenger traffic; Goods: 1.7.1964.
Sections of the two platforms, largely covered in vegetation alongside the Strawberry Line pedestrian and cycle way, are the sole remaining station structures. Early railway cottages erected for the station master and a ganger, incorporating Bristol & Exeter Railway style bargeboards, continue in residential use alongside the A370, west of the station. One of these is today called 'Station Cottage'. A separate station master's house dating from the 1930s, this time on the village side of the line, stands alongside the former station approach road. It continues in private residential use, well hidden behind a high fence and vegetation. A modern housing development on nearby Station Close is a further reminder of the earlier era.

COSSINGTON   ST 358408

Opened: 21.7.1890 with the opening of the Bridgwater branch of the Somerset & Dorset Railway, Edington Junction – Bridgwater North.
Closed: Passengers: 1.12.1952 with closure of the branch to passenger traffic; Goods: 4.10.1954.
Today the station buildings are in residential use on Station Road, the two storey stone station master's house being 'The Old Station House' and the attached single storey building, with an extension, being 'Station Cottage'. Three large houses erected in 1989/90 stand on a section of the trackbed and goods yard. An old ground frame hut originally sited on the platform close to the station master's house has been moved to the East Somerset Railway at Cranmore.

CRANMORE   ST 668430

Opened: 9.11.1858 with the opening of the Witham – Shepton Mallet section of the East Somerset Railway.
Closed: Passengers: 9.9.1963 with closure of the Yatton to Witham line to passenger traffic; Goods: 17.1.1966.
Reopened 4.4.1980 when trains began running on the restored East Somerset Railway as far as Merryfield Lane. Soon after the line closed to passengers in 1963, the down (south) side shelter was demolished but the platform survived and is now covered in vegetation. The station site was taken over by the East Somerset Railway with the support of David Sheppard, the renowned artist of railway and animal subjects. The East Somerset Railway Centre opened at Cranmore in 1975 but the first train did not run until 1980. A new house was constructed in 1974 behind the up platform and east

of the surviving main building; this continues in residential use 'New Station House' but is not associated with the East Somerset Railway operation. In 1991 a large new building was opened behind the east end of the surviving up (north) side platform. Materials for its construction came from the former Lodge Hill station (on the Cheddar Valley line west of Cheddar) and also the Wells Priory Road goods shed. The two storey building which, in 1994 received an Ian Allan Heritage Award, incorporates a large café, 'The Whistlestop', on the ground floor and a book/model/souvenir shop and booking office at platform level. The surviving former up platform has been extended to accommodate a five carriage train.

Between the new house and the original main building the small wooden structure is a former bookstall from Salisbury station. West of the main building is a cast iron gent's urinal which is still in use; it replaced an earlier wooden structure. The original main building which contained the booking office, waiting room and station master's office now houses a small museum. Also on the platform is a rare 1926 telephone box. On the down side beyond the west end of the platform is the surviving Cranmore signal box (closed in May 1963) which is used for exhibitions. West of the box is an operating miniature railway, which began running in June 2009.

To the west of the station site, on the up side, sheds and workshops have been erected for restoration and maintenance of locomotives and rolling stock. The workshop originated at Devonport Dockyard and smoke vents came from a former shed at Westbury. A short distance behind the up side the large former station master's house continues in residential use, 'Station House'. Today Cranmore station is the active base of the restored East Somerset Railway which operates steam and diesel hauled passenger services at various times throughout the year.

CRANMORE WEST   ST 663428

Opened: 4.4.1980 with the opening of the Cranmore – Merryfield Lane section of the East Somerset Railway.
Closed: Remains open for services on the East Somerset Railway.
A short distance to the west of Cranmore station, close to the workshops, this is a simple concrete platform on the down side of the restored East Somerset Railway. To the rear of the platform is a wire fence and concrete posts. Three seats are provided on the platform but no shelter. A further seat is alongside the short access path.

CREECH ST MICHAEL HALT   ST 272254

Opened: 13.8.1928 on the Bridgwater – Taunton section of the Great Western Railway originally opened on 1.7.1842.
Closed: 5.10.1964.
Today no evidence of the halt remains at trackside. Minor changes in the brickwork on the west side of the adjacent road over bridge probably indicate where the down side access path left the road. A section of railway style fencing lines the west side of the road south of the bridge.

CREWKERNE   ST 453086

Opened: 19.7.1860 with the opening of the Yeovil Junction – Exeter section of the London & South Western Railway.
Closed: Passengers: remains open for services on the London (Waterloo) – Yeovil – Exeter line; Goods: 18.4.1966
Extensive renovation work has been undertaken, in particular in the early 1990s, and today Crewkerne is one of the most impressive stations remaining open in Somerset. When visited in June 2010 the three storey station master's house, integrated in the main building on the up side, was occupied by an accountancy firm.

Only the former up platform remains in use on the now single track section. The former down platform remains in place but the shelter has gone as has the footbridge, though its two supporting legs remain adjacent to the road bridge south of the station. The 1960 signal box beyond the east end of the up platform survives though unused and derelict. Much of the former goods yard on the Crewkerne side of the station is occupied by Bradford Building Supplies, the former goods shed being used for vehicle maintenance. The former weighbridge house beside the entrance to the station approach remains in place.

CROWCOMBE HEATHFIELD   ST 137342

Opened: 31.3.1862 with the opening of the West Somerset Railway, Norton Junction – Watchet. *Opened as Crowcombe Heathfield but from 1.12.1889 was renamed Crowcombe to avoid confusion with Heathfield station in Devon.*
Closed: Passengers: 4.1.1971 with closure of the Minehead branch, Norton Junction – Minehead; Goods: 6.7.1964.
Reopened. 9.6.1979 with the opening of the Stogumber – Bishops Lydeard section of the restored West Somerset Railway. *Renamed Crowcombe Heathfield in 1991.*
Following the reopening of the station on the West Somerset Railway, one of the first developments was the replacement of the former wooden waiting shelter on the 1891 down platform which had been demolished in 1967. Initially this was replaced by a former GWR bow ended corrugated hut which had served as a goods office at Flax Bourton. A new wooden waiting shelter was purchased and brought into use from Easter Monday, 8th April 1996. The Flax Bourton hut was transferred to a site behind and above the up platform at the Bishops Lydeard end and, following refurbishment, is now used as a store.
The Grade II listed main station building on the original 1862 up platform, now containing the booking office and small buffet, has been recently renovated, officially opening for business on 25th June 2010. At its south end a new toilet building with disabled facilities had been added in 2004. For some 15 years after reopening only single line working operated through Crowcombe but from May 1994 the crossing loop was reintroduced. A signal box transferred from Ebbw Vale in South Wales some eight years earlier came into use replacing the earlier 1879 box closed in 1967 and subsequently destroyed by fire. Of a typical GWR 1930s style, it incorporates equipment from a number of old boxes, in particular that at Frome North Junction. Other 2010

features of the station include a lamp hut on the up platform adjacent to the renovated building relocated from Meads Crossing at Huntsworth and old style lampposts re-sited like those at Bishops Lydeard from the Tiverton Junction station. The base of the former goods office, south of the main building, can be seen beneath one of the platform seats. On the down platform is a display of permanent way equipment and rails, including a section of Brunel's 7ft gauge track as used on the line between 1862 and 1882. Behind this platform adjacent to the new shelter is a greenhouse presented to the station to assist in the tending of the attractive gardens.

Because of its attractive setting, Crowcombe Heathfield has been used several times as a film location including the 1997 film 'The Land Girls'. A housing development has been developed on the down side north of the station alongside the former goods siding. The name 'Bakers Orchard' reflects the use of the site by the Bakers Lorry yard and depot. The 1862 station master's house at the Minehead end, complete with traditional Bristol & Exeter barge boards and now known as 'Puff Cottage', continues in residential use.

DONIFORD BEACH HALT   ST 085429

Opened: 27.6.1987 on the Blue Anchor – Williton section of the West Somerset Railway originally reopened on 28.8.1976.
Closed: remains open for services on the restored West Somerset Railway.
A late addition to Somerset's stations and halts, it was opened by the West Somerset Railway in June 1987. The platform is constructed of pre-cast concrete sections from the closed Montacute station on the Yeovil – Taunton line. A GWR pagoda style corrugated iron shelter from the closed Cove Halt on the former Exe Valley line in Devon has been restored and erected on the platform.

DONYATT HALT   ST 342140

Opened: 5.5.1928 on the Taunton – Chard branch of the Bristol & Exeter Railway originally opened on 11.9.1866.
Closed: 10.9.1962 with closure of the Taunton – Chard Junction line to passenger traffic.
Also temporary closure 5.2.1951 to 7.5.1951 due to the fuel crises.
In 2002 the only surviving feature to be seen was a section of the former wooden platform face partly hidden by undergrowth. Behind the former halt was a number of war-time concrete traps, again partially in undergrowth. A repeat visit in June 2010 found a remarkable transformation with a reconstructed platform built alongside a cycleway/footpath laid on the former trackbed. This is part of the National Cycle Network, known as the 'Stop Line Way' as it follows the line of war-time concrete traps laid across country between the English and Bristol Channels. These traps are still prominent behind the restored halt. On the platform is a new wooden hut, a nameboard and a small statue of Doreen, a war time evacuee to the area, whose story is told on a display board. To the south of the halt is a distant signal.

DRAYCOTT   ST 474507

Opened: 5.4.1870 with the opening of the Cheddar – Wells section of the Cheddar Valley & Yatton Railway.
Closed: Passengers: 9.9.1963 with closure of the Yatton – Witham line to passenger traffic; Goods: 9.3.1963.
Both the station building and station master's house remain in residential use on Station Road, the former still displaying 'Draycott Station' on the trackside façade and retaining its Bristol & Exeter Railway barge boards, now painted brown. The platform edge remains visible. The station house features Bristol & Exeter style cruciform design ridge tiles. A new house 'Level Crossing' stands to the west of 'Station House' adjacent to the site of the level crossing on Back Lane. The nearby former 'Railway Inn' is now 'Strawberry Special' reflecting the name given to the former Yatton – Wells line.

DULVERTON   SS 927256

Opened: 1.11.1873 with the opening of the Wiveliscombe – Barnstaple section of the Devon & Somerset Railway.
Closed: Passengers: 3.10.1966 with closure of the Norton Junction - Barnstaple line to passenger traffic; Goods: 6.7.1964.
Following the station's closure in 1966 the station site was taken over by the large Carnarvon Arms Hotel alongside the Station Approach. This hotel had been built by Lord Carnarvon to serve visitors travelling to the area by train for local fishing and to view the Exmoor scenery. The site was levelled and grassed over with the station buildings converted for use as staff accommodation. The goods shed was also used by the hotel.

Visiting in early 2002 the author found the whole site up for sale as well as the hotel, which was closed. Notices indicated that the site was to be auctioned with planning permission granted for 'residential use and as a bistro'. For a few years there was no action but a re-visit in August 2010 revealed a complete transformation. The former hotel is now a series of apartments and the station building and goods shed have been converted into private houses; the remainder of the site is now laid out as a splendid garden. The whole complex is clearly one of the best examples of the re-use of a station site in Somerset and indeed the South West.

DUNBALL   ST 313410

Opened: c June 1873 on the Bristol – Bridgwater section of the GWR originally opened on 14.6.1841.
Closed: Passengers: 5.10.1964; Goods: 2.11.1964.
No trace remains at trackside of the buildings and staggered platforms that were sited north (down side) and south (up side) of the bridge over the King's Sedgemoor Drain. Station Road still runs east towards the site from the A38.

DUNKERTON   ST 718594

Opened: 9.5.1910 with the opening of the Cam Valley line, Camerton – Limpley Stoke.
Closed: Passengers: 21.9.1925 with closure of the Cam Valley line to passenger traffic; Goods: 15.2.1951 with complete closure of the line.

Also temporary closures: Passengers: 22.3.1915 to 9.7.1923; Goods: 1.4.1918 to 9.7.1923 originally as war-time measures. When viewed from an adjacent road to the north no identifiable remains of the station could be seen apart from isolated rubble. The former station access road south-west of a surviving road over bridge parapet was readily apparent but access to it was barred by a locked gate and barbed wire.

DUNKERTON COLLIERY HALT   ST 695585

Opened: 9.10.1911 on the Cam Valley line, Camerton – Limpley Stoke originally opened 9.5.1910.
Closed: 21.9.1925 with closure of the Cam Valley line to passenger traffic.
Also temporary closure 22.3.1915 to 9.7.1923 originally as a war-time measure.
Today the cutting in which the halt was sited, west of a road over bridge, has been infilled. The unusual shaped bridge survives however and on its south side two former rail track sections, covered in ivy, form posts and mark the top of the former access path down to the halt. A new metal kissing gate is in front of the two posts by the road side.

DUNSTER   SS 997448

Opened: 16.7.1874 with the opening of the Minehead Railway, Minehead – Watchet.
Closed: Passengers: 4.1.1971 with closure of the Minehead branch, Norton Junction – Minehead; Goods: 6.7.1964.
Re-opened: 28.3.1976 with the opening of the Minehead – Blue Anchor section of the restored West Somerset Railway. Since its re-opening in 1976, extensive restoration and renovation has taken place at one of the most attractive stations on the West Somerset Railway (WSR). The main station building is now Grade II listed. It receives visitors to the tourist attractions of Dunster village and castle. The annual December 'Dunster by Candlelight' event in the village brings a large number of passengers to the station. The old booking office has been restored and the toilets are original.

The former parcels office houses a Waterlow ticket printing machine purchased from British Rail at Crewe. This has been restored to working order and is now used to print Edmondson card tickets for use on the West Somerset Railway and other heritage lines. Over six million such tickets have been printed including the special souvenir tickets for the first train through the Channel Tunnel. The Grade II listed 1874 goods shed, which underwent major repairs to the roof in 1992, is used by the WSR's permanent way department. The only surviving loading gauge on the WSR is over the doors at the Taunton end of the shed. Both the station building and the goods shed were used in the past by the Hornby company as the template for its model of a country station and goods shed.

DURSTON   ST 307283

Opened: 1.10.1853 with the opening of the Durston – Yeovil Hendford branch from the Bristol & Exeter Railway to passenger traffic. Goods traffic commenced on 26.10.1853.
Closed: Passengers: 5.10.1964 soon after closure of the

Durston – Yeovil line, it continued to serve passengers on the main Bristol – Taunton line for a short period; Goods: 6.7.1964.

No significant remains of this junction station survive apart from a section of railings on the down (east) side opposite the former 'Railway Hotel', now in residential use. The former Railway Cottages alongside the former down side approach road also continue in residential use, the end house being named 'Station House'; this name being on a plaque in the shape of an engine. The house also has a roof top locomotive shaped weather vane. The adjoining house is called 'Turntable Cottage'. The site of the former up side goods yard was, in August 2010, behind locked gates. The trackbed of the former branch line to Yeovil is derelict.

EBDON LANE HALT   ST 370643
Opened 1.12.1897 with the opening of the Weston-super-Mare – Clevedon section of the Weston, Clevedon & Portishead Light Railway.
Closed: 20.5.1940 with closure of the line.
No trace of the halt, at which there was a small wooden shelter but no platform, can now be seen.

EDINGTON BURTLE   ST 391429
Opened: 4.1856 on the Highbridge Wharf – Glastonbury section of the Somerset Central Railway originally opened on 28.8.1854. *Opened as Edington Road, changed to Edington Junction with opening of Bridgwater branch in 1890 and finally to Edington Burtle with branch closure in 1953.*
Closed: Passengers: 7.3.1966 with closure of the Evercreech Junction – Highbridge line to passenger traffic; Goods: 13.7.1964.

Following closure of the station in 1966 most of the site, in particular the former goods yard, was taken over by the National Rivers Authority, now the Environment Agency. The station master's house, east of the station 'Station House', has been modernised and extended with some of the former trackbed incorporated into the garden. Though cut back by some 100 ft a section of the former island platform survives, though the majority is covered by bushes and undergrowth.

  The former 'Railway Hotel', north-east of the station was renamed 'The Tom Mogg Inn', after one of the station's last signalmen/porters. The original sign showing him holding the Somerset Central Railway handbell ringing at the level crossing in earlier times had, by 2010, been replaced by an illustration of him with a red flag, tray and beer mug! One of the former level crossing gates at the east end of the station site is now at the Somerset & Dorset Railway Trust's site at Washford on the West Somerset Railway.

EVERCREECH JUNCTION   ST 639365
Opened: 3.2.1862 with the opening of the Glastonbury – Cole section of the Somerset Central Railway. *Opened as Evercreech, the suffix Junction added when the Bath Extension of the Somerset & Dorset Railway opened in 1874.*
Closed: Passengers: 7.3.1966 with closure of the Bath – Poole line to passenger traffic; Goods: 29.11.1965.

The station master's house and the former station building on the down (north) side of the line both survive today in residential use. The up platform buildings were demolished in February 1968 and a garage built on the platform, accessed between the two surviving buildings. The former trackbed has been infilled. Industrial units have been erected in the former down side goods yard, known in 2010 as Evercreech Junction Industrial Estate. The former Railway Hotel immediately south of the station was initially renamed 'The Silent Whistle' but is now 'The Natterjack'.

EVERCREECH NEW   ST 645386
Opened: 20.7.1874 with the opening of the Bath Extension of the Somerset & Dorset Railway, Evercreech Junction – Bath. *Opened as Evercreech Village, renamed Evercreech New two months later.*
Closed: Passengers: 7.3.1966 with closure of the Bath – Poole line to passenger traffic; Goods: 1.7.1964.

The station was demolished in 1968/69 and the entire site redeveloped for housing, Kiln Drive on the former goods yard and Westbrook Road over the remainder. A short section of railway railings, originally behind the up platform, survives alongside a parking area adjacent to no. 33 Westbrook Road. Station Way, a cul-de-sac off Weymouth Road, generally follows the alignment of the former station approach road leading to the south end of the down platform. Remains of a rail over bridge abutment can be seen to the north of the station site on the north side of Leighton Lane.

FARRINGTON GURNEY HALT   ST 638553
Opened : 11.7.1927 on the Bristol – Radstock line originally opened on 3.9.1873.
Closed: 2.11.1959 with closure of the Bristol – Radstock line to passenger traffic.
Today all traces of the halt have gone, the cutting in which it stood being infilled. The road over bridge to the west has gone and the road realigned. With no ticket office on the platform, tickets were issued through a small window at the nearby Miners Arms public house. This window remains with an explanatory notice above in the side wall of what is now the 'Spice Dunes Indian Restaurant'.

FLAX BOURTON
First Station   ST 517697
Opened: 1.9.1860 on the Bristol – Taunton section of the Bristol & Exeter Railway originally opened on 14.6.1841. *Opened as Bourton and renamed Flax Bourton 1.9.1893.*
Closed: 1.3.1893 (see second station)
There are no trackside remains of this station but the station master's house continues in residential use on Clevedon Road (B3130). The eastern section of the building which has Bristol & Exeter style barge boards, is called 'Station Cottage'.
Second Station   ST 513698
Opened: 2.3.1893 replacing the first station which was ¼ mile to the east.
Closed: Passengers: 2.12.1963; Goods: 1.7.1964.

A derelict section of the brick up side building stands at the end of the former station approach road which is now a private road serving housing. Also at the end of the road adjacent to the line is the derelict goods shed with a section of canopy surviving on the road side.

FRESHFORD   ST 791603

Opened: 2.2.1857 with the opening of the Wilts, Somerset & Weymouth Railway branch, Bradford Junction – Bathampton.
Closed: Passengers: remains open for services on the Bristol – Weymouth line; Goods: 10.6.1963.
Considerable renovation has taken place in recent years with the situation much improved since the author visited the station in 2002. Modern metal and glass shelters and new lighting are provided on both platforms, connected by a modern metal footbridge. The problem of the required high step from the up platform onto the train, the consequence of cant on the curved track, was solved in 2006 by the raising in height of the platform surface. The 2010 flower beds are well tended and a gravel area, behind which is an old style nameboard, has been laid out on the site of the former down side building. Limited sections of old railings and gate posts survive at the down side entrance from Station Road. The station master's house on this road continues in residential use, 'Old Station House'.

FROME   ST 785476

Opened: 7.10.1850 as the terminus of the Westbury (Wilts) – Frome section of the Wilts, Somerset & Weymouth Railway.
Closed: Passengers: Remains open principally for trains on the Bristol – Weymouth line, also limited peak hour services to and from London (Paddington). Goods: 1967.
Decline set in from 31st December 1959 when the last passenger train left Frome for Bristol via the Radstock line. The engine shed closed in September 1963 and, most significantly, the track was singled through the station on 19th August 1970, only the up platform (towards Westbury) remaining in use. The up bay platform was taken out of use as from 17th May 1971. The footbridge was no longer needed and was removed.

By the early 1970s, the whole station structure was in a bad condition and the train shed needed to be propped up with a steel post. With large costs likely for renovation, British Rail proposed complete demolition with replacement of the train shed by a bus shelter structure. Public outcry led to the station being listed as a Grade II Building of Architectural and Historic Interest. A number of major renovation initiatives have been undertaken and today the station has the last surviving example of an overall Brunel type wooden roof.

When visited in early July 2010, the main wooden building was in reasonable condition, there being evidence of recent painting. The overall train shed was however showing some signs of neglect. The waiting room behind the former up platform was in good condition, the booking office hours being 0625-1215 hrs Monday to Saturday Passengers are provided with three GWR seats on the platform. The former down platform and waiting room remain in place but unused.

A notice on the wall above this platform indicates that under the Network Rail Community Scheme the area is being enhanced by Frome Station Friends, in partnership with Network Rail.

Much of the area surrounding the station has been redeveloped – the creamery has closed, the site being used by a builders' merchants (Jewsons) and the malting building demolished except for a section of the rear wall. Both the former enterprises had operated in conjunction with the railway. The site of the engine shed and much of the goods yard, including the site of the demolished goods shed on the up side, are used by Focus and a number of other retail/industrial units. The 1882 station master's house remains in residential use while the nearby former Railway Hotel called 'The First and Last' in 2002 is now the 'Tong Dynasty Chinese restaurant'.

GLASTONBURY AND STREET   ST 490390

Opened: 28.8.1854 as the terminus of the Highbridge Wharf – Glastonbury section of the Somerset Central Railway. *The suffix 'and Street' was added in July 1886.*
Closed: Passengers and Goods: 7.3.1966 with closure of the Evercreech Junction – Highbridge line to passenger traffic. Following closure in 1966, the station remained largely intact until 1984 when the buildings were demolished and the site cleared. The island platform canopy survived however and was moved to the St John's car park in the centre of Glastonbury, rescued by the Glastonbury Conservation Society. This project was awarded second prize in a national 'Pride of Place' competition in 1984.

Much of the station site is now used by a variety of commercial/industrial uses but the former engineers' offices are now a private dwelling, 'Railway Cottage' (on a plaque with an engine motif). Renovated level crossing gates and posts stand where the railway lines (from Evercreech Junction and the Wells branch) entered the station site. Much of the former goods yard is occupied by Snows Timber whose administrative offices are in The Pollards, a large red building south-east of the station, which was built in 1861 as the 'Abbey Arms and Railway Hotel'. Part of the building was leased to the Somerset Central Railway (later Somerset & Dorset Railway) which used it as its headquarters until this was transferred to Bath in 1877.

HALLATROW   ST 633572

Opened: 3.9.1873 with the opening of the Bristol & North Somerset Railway, Bristol – Radstock.
Closed: Passengers: 2.11.1959 with closure of the Bristol – Radstock – Frome line to passenger traffic; Goods: 15.6.1964.
Today a number of the significant features of the station are still in place, over 50 years after it closed to passengers. The main building, including the horizontal canopy, is now part of a large house, 'The Ticket Office', with a separate but linked, modern structure on the former trackbed. The former goods yard, north of the station, is now the 'Old Station Business Park' with ten units. At the shared entrance to the house and business park from the A39 are two substantial

former railway gate posts and a short section of railway style railings. Remnants of the former platforms south of the station can be seen leading towards the bridge which carries the A39 over the former trackbed. South of this bridge housing covers the former trackbed. To the south-west of the bridge the station master's house continues in residential use, 'Station House'. South-east of the bridge 'The Old Station' public house is the revised name of the former Railway Hotel. An old railway carriage in its rear garden is now used as a restaurant.

HAM GREEN HALT   ST 536755

Opened: 23.12.1926 on the Portishead branch originally opened on 18.4.1867
Closed: 7.9.1964 with closure of the Portishead branch to passenger traffic.
Built to serve the residents of Ham Green village and more significantly for visitors to the former Ham Green isolation hospital, part of the old single platform can still be seen on, and adjacent to, Ham Green viaduct over which freight trains now run to and from the Royal Portbury Docks over a section of the former Portishead branch.

HAM LANE HALT   ST 385668

Opened: 1.12.1897 with the opening of the Weston-super-Mare – Clevedon section of the Weston, Clevedon & Portishead Light Railway.
Closed: 20.5.1940 with closure of the line.
No trace of this halt, at which there was a small wooden hut but no platform, can now be seen.

HAMPTON ROW HALT   ST 761659

Opened: 18.3.1907 on the Bath – Chippenham section of the GWR Bristol – London line originally opened on 30.6.1841.
Closed: 29.4.1917.
No trace, or indeed a photo of this short-lived halt on the eastern edge of Bath, now exists. The road, Hampton Row, has a number of derelict houses at its eastern end close to an existing footbridge over the main London line adjacent to the site of the halt.

HATCH   ST 304204

Opened: 11.9.1866 with the opening of the Taunton – Chard branch from the Bristol & Exeter Railway.
Closed: Passengers: 10.9.1962 with closure of the Taunton – Chard Junction line to passenger traffic; Goods: 6.7.1964. Also temporary closure to all traffic 5.2.1951 to 7.5.1951 due to the fuel crisis.
The station building and goods shed survive now occupied by a stone/masonry firm, Sterling Services. The station building has been partially renovated with the canopy and brackets remaining in place. The site is accessed from Station Road alongside which is a section of railway style railing and an old kissing gate from which a tarmac path still runs down the side of the cutting into the station site.

HENSTRIDGE   ST 726202

Opened: 10.9.1863 with the opening of the Blandford St Mary – Blandford – Templecombe section of the Somerset & Dorset Railway.
Closed: Passengers: 7.3.1966 with closure of the Bath – Poole line to passenger traffic; Goods: 5.4.1965.
The station building and part of the platform were demolished in 1968; in the mid 1990s the remaining section of the platform was demolished and the whole station site, together with land behind to the west, was redeveloped for housing including one road, Old Station Gardens. A house close to the site of the station is named, 'The Halt', whilst another to the north on the former goods yard is appropriately, 'The Sidings'.
Immediately to the south of the station was a level crossing with Blackmoor Lane. All four posts of the crossing remain as does the gate on the north side. Remnants of the southern gate lie in the undergrowth. The station agent's (master's) house to the west of the level crossing continues in residential use, 'Station House'. A gravel pedestrian path follows the alignment of the former trackbed north from the former level crossing towards a surviving road over bridge carrying the A30.

HIGHBRIDGE AND BURNHAM   ST 322470

Opened: 14.6.1841 with the opening of the Bristol – Bridgwater section of the Bristol & Exeter Railway. *Opened as Highbridge and renamed a number of times: Highbridge West 5.5.1950, Highbridge for Burnham-on-Sea 30.6 1962, Highbridge 6.5.1974 and Highbridge & Burnham 17.5.1991.*
Closed: Passengers: Remains open served by local services on the Bristol – Taunton – Exeter line, also limited peak hour services to and from London (Paddington); Goods: 2.11.1964.
Today little remains of the original station structures apart from sections of railings and gates on the up (towards Bristol) platform, the main buildings being demolished in the 1970s. The goods shed within the yard on the up side north of the road bridge has gone and the site is unused. Modern metal and glass shelters serve passengers on both platforms and an additional 'bus stop' style shelter on the up platform contains cycle stands, all of which were in use when seen in July 2010. The concrete footbridge, which replaced an earlier structure, links the platforms at the north end; it is truncated on the down side as the original extension to the demolished Somerset & Dorset station has gone.
There is a small garden on the down platform and in the 1990s the area adjacent to the station approach on the up side was enhanced with a new car park and small public park with seats. To the west of this park is a small housing development accessed by Station Walk. The former Railway Hotel west of the station, a former 18th century coaching inn (indicated by a wall plaque), has been demolished and replaced by 'Alpha House' that incorporates the library.

HIGHBRIDGE EAST (S & D)   ST 323469

Opened: 28.8.1854 with the opening of the Highbridge Wharf – Glastonbury section of the Somerset Central

Railway. *The suffix 'East' was added from 26.9.1949.*
Closed: Passengers: 7.3.1966 with closure of the Evercreech Junction - Highbridge line to passenger traffic; Goods: 2.11.1964.

Following closure in 1966 the station buildings were demolished in December 1970 and, up to the mid 1980s, the former up (south) concrete platform could still be seen. In 2002, when the author previously visited, the entire station site was covered in rubble and soil. The truncated concrete footbridge linked to the GWR station was the only remaining clue to the presence of the Somerset & Dorset station. The site has now been redeveloped for housing, accessed appropriately by Somerset Way and Dorset Close. The former S & D line towards Burnham-on-Sea and the goods yard west of the GWR line have been redeveloped for housing (Southwell Crescent), a car park and supermarket.

ILMINSTER   ST 348150
Opened : 11.9.1866 with the opening of the Taunton – Chard branch from the Bristol & Exeter Railway.
Closed: Passengers: 10.9.1962 with closure of the Taunton – Chard Junction line to passenger traffic; Goods: 6.7.1964. Also temporary closure to all traffic 5.2.1951 to 7.5.1951 due to a fuel crisis.

The station building and goods shed both survive in good condition within the Westcombe Trading Estate. In June 2010 the station building was used by the Glamour Pets Parlour whilst the goods shed had two occupants: a carpet showroom, The Carpet Shed, and agricultural engineers, McCormack/GA Vowles Ltd. The former station master's house continues in residential use on Station Road. The former Railway Hotel, also on Station Road, has gone.

ILTON HALT   ST 343170
Opened: 26.5.1928 on the Taunton – Chard line originally opened on 11.9.1866
Closed: 10.9.1962 with closure of the Taunton – Chard Junction line to passenger traffic.
Also temporary closure 5.2.1951 to 7.5.1951 due to fuel crisis.

There is now no trace of the halt on the embankment, though the access path from the road linking Ilton village to the A358 remains. A large pill box sited beyond the north end of the halt site is still there, as are a number of concrete posts that ran parallel to the track opposite the platform.

KEINTON MANDEVILLE   ST 565305
Opened: 1.7.1905 with the opening of the Castle Cary – Charlton Mackrell section of the GWR cut off line Castle Cary - Cogload Junction.
Closed: Passengers and Goods: 10.9.1962 with the withdrawal of local passenger services between Castle Cary and Taunton.
The site of the station itself and the goods yard on the up side are now largely occupied by a car scrap yard, Cross Keys Motor Services. Small sections of the building and platform on the down side survive.

KELSTON   ST 689670
Opened: 1.12.1869 on the Mangotsfield – Bath branch from the Bristol – Gloucester line originally opened four months earlier on 4.8.1869.
Closed: 1.1.1949
Today, more than 60 years after its closed, no significant remains of the station can be seen alongside what is now the Bristol – Bath Cycleway (National Cycle Network No 4), which runs along the former trackbed. Raised banks either side of the cycleway indicate the sites of the former platforms and limited rubble could derive from the former buildings. A footpath to the bridge over the River Avon from the station, with railings alongside, is still there behind vegetation on the north-east side of the cycleway..

KEYNSHAM   ST 658689
Opened: 31.8.1840 with the opening of the Bristol – Bath section of the GWR Bristol – London line. *Suffix 'and Somerdale' applied 1.2.1925 to 6.5.1974.*
Closed: Passengers: remains open for local services on the Bristol to Bath line; Goods: 29.11.1965.
Following a reprieve from possible closure in November 1969, the principal buildings were demolished in June 1970. The 1930s platform canopies at the west end of the platform survived. The fine covered footbridge, dismantled in May 1970, was re-erected at Buckfastleigh on the South Devon Railway. A December 1985 joint project by British Rail and Avon County Council included a new footbridge, a brick shelter on the up (towards Bath) platform and an extended car park, which is now a pay and display facility. Ramped steps from the footbridge serve the up side but only normal steps link to the down platform, an issue of concern to passengers. The down platform has no shelter. A small hut serving as a booking office, initially at the base of the down platform steps and subsequently relocated to the top by the road bridge, reflects the importance of Keynsham as a commuter station for Bath and Bristol. Today the station is virtually that following the 1985 renovation. The goods shed, east of the station on the down side, closed some 45 years ago, survives, occupied in mid 2010 by a vehicle repair firm.

KINGSTON ROAD HALT   ST 391682
Opened: 1.12.1897 with the opening of the Weston-super-Mare – Clevedon section of the Weston, Clevedon & Portishead Light Railway.
Closed: 20.5.1940 with closure of the line.
No trace of the halt, at which there was a small shelter but no platform, can now be seen.

LANGFORD   ST 473607
Opened: 4.12.1901 with the opening of the Wrington Vale Light Railway, Congresbury – Blagdon.
Closed: Passengers: 14.9.1931 with closure of the Wrington Vale Light Railway to passenger traffic; Goods: 1.11.1950 with closure of the Wrington – Blagdon section of the line to goods traffic.
The station building was demolished in 1958 but remnants

of the platform survive beneath undergrowth alongside a track running north-west from the A38, close to Yew Tree Close. The 1903 station master's house on the south-east side of the road continues in residential use with major alterations and extensions. For many years a level crossing gate lay in the hedge on the north-west side of the A38 but in about 2002 this was wrecked, apparently in a road accident, and removed.

LANGPORT EAST   ST 423272
Opened: 2.7.1906 on the Curry Rivel Junction – Somerton section of the GWR cut off route Castle Cary – Cogload Junction originally opened for goods traffic to and from the west on 12.2.1906.
Closed: Passengers and Goods: 10.9.1962 with the withdrawal of local passenger services between Castle Cary – Taunton.
Following closure in 1906, the buildings stood for over 20 years. Today the only visible evidence is a section of old railings and the base of the building on the down side (towards Taunton) on the north side of Eastover Road. To the north of the line, which still carries main line Paddington to West of England trains, the station site has been redeveloped for housing but a long section of railway style railings alongside the former access road to the up side is still there.

LANGPORT WEST   ST 414265
Opened: 1.10.1853 with the opening to passenger traffic of the Durston – Yeovil Hendford branch from the Bristol & Exeter Railway. *Suffix 'West' added from 2.7.1906 when Langport East station opened.*
Closed: Passengers: 15.6.1964 with closure of Taunton – Yeovil line to passenger traffic; Goods: 6.7.1964 with closure of Taunton – Yeovil line to all traffic.
Today the Westover Trading Estate on the western edge of the town covers the former site of the station and goods yard. The sole remnant from the railway era is a former warehouse in the goods yard with an extension, the building now called 'Great Western House'. The road over bridge at the north end of the station site carrying the A378 remains and can be viewed from within the trading estate.

LODGE HILL   ST 499484
Opened: 5.4.1870 with the opening of the Cheddar – Wells section of the Cheddar Valley & Yatton Railway.
Closed: Passengers: 9.9.1963 with closure of the Yatton – Witham line to passenger traffic; Goods: 10.6.1963.
Lodge Hill Business Park, linked to Westbury-sub-Mendip village to the north by Station Road, now covers the former station site. The station building, for a period used as an activity centre by Bristol Grammar School, has now gone but the former goods shed, complete with road side canopy, survives used, in 2010, by industrial and commercial firms including the business park office. Materials from the demolished station building were used in the construction of the large new building at Cranmore for the East Somerset Railway. The former station sign is now at the Great Western

Society Museum at Didcot. The adjacent road over bridge east of the station site remains today.

LONG ASHTON   ST 549700
Opened: 12.7.1926 on the Bristol – Bridgwater section of the GWR originally opened on 14.6.1841. *Suffix Platform until 23.9.1929.*
Closed: 6.10.1941.
Some 70 years after its closure, no trace remains of this halt on an embankment west of Bristol. At the time of writing in early 2011 there are some calls for a new station to be opened at or close to the old site, if the proposed new stadium for Bristol City Football Club and associated new Arena are built in the near future.

LONG SUTTON & PITNEY   ST 455270
Opened: 1.10.1907 on the Curry Rivel Junction – Somerton section of the GWR cut off line Castle Cary – Cogload Junction, originally opened for goods traffic to and from the west on 12.2.1906.
Closed: Passengers: 10.9.1962 with the withdrawal of local passenger services between Castle Cary and Taunton; Goods: 6.7.1964.
A small section of the platform on the down (towards Taunton) side west of the high road over bridge is the only surviving trackside remnant. The station master's house continues in residential use, 'Station House' on the east side of the road north from the A372 (Hermitage Road). Small sections of fencing in the hedgerow indicate the probable location of the former path to the down side platform.

LYNG HALT   ST 332288
Opened: 24.9.1928 on the Durston – Yeovil branch line originally opened on 1.10.1853.
Closed: 15.6.1964 with closure of the Taunton – Yeovil line to passenger traffic.
Remains of an old gate that was at the road side entrance to the access path to the single platform can just be seen in the hedge at the east end of the road over bridge. Two concrete posts in the former cutting, just visible in 2002, could not be seen on the 2010 visit.

MARSTON MAGNA   ST 600223
Opened: 1.9.1856 with the opening of the Frome – Yeovil section of the Wilts, Somerset & Weymouth Railway.
Closed: Passengers: 3.10.1966; Goods: 5.11.1962.
The station buildings and platforms were demolished soon after closure. Sections of railings behind the north end of the down (towards Yeovil) platform remain close to a garage that stands approximately on the site of the down side building. The station master's house, also on the down side, continues in residential use with extensions, 'Chartwell House'.

MARTOCK   ST 462201
Opened: 1.10.1853 with the opening to passenger traffic of the Durston – Yeovil Hendford branch from the Bristol & Exeter Railway.

Closed: Passengers: 15.6.1964 with closure of the Taunton –
Yeovil line to passenger traffic; Goods: 6.7.1964.
Today an industrial estate, 'Martock Business Park' covers
both the station site and also sidings that served the
adjoining gas works. Isolated remnants of railway related
walls survive. One of the roads serving the industrial units is
called Great Western Road. The Railway Hotel on Coat Road,
close to the former site on the village side, displays a plaque
recording its link with the long gone railway era. When
viewed in July 2010, the hotel was derelict, surrounded by a
mesh fence; the plaque was however still on the front wall.

MASBURY   ST 603472

Opened: 20.7.1874 with the opening of the Bath Extension of
the Somerset & Dorset Railway, Evercreech Junction – Bath.
Closed: Passengers: 7.3.1966 with closure of the Bath – Poole
line to passenger traffic; Goods: 10.6.1963.
The station master's house at the south end of the former up
(towards Bath) platform continues in residential use with an
extension at its northern end over the site of the old signal
box. The former platforms and trackbed are incorporated
into a large garden. The building at the north end of the up
platform, which formerly incorporated the booking office and
the waiting rooms, survives, including the chimney, but in
June 2010 appeared to be derelict. Remnants of access steps
to each platform from either side of the road over bridge
north of the station can still just be seen in the extensive
vegetation alongside the road.

MELLS ROAD   ST 714513

Opened: 4.3.1887 on the Radstock – Frome line originally
opened for coal traffic on 14.11.1854 and passenger traffic
on 5.7.1875. *Suffix 'Road' added 16.11.1898.*
Closed: 2.11.1959 with closure of the Bristol – Radstock –
Frome line to passenger traffic; Goods: 15.6.1964.
Today one disused track on the former Radstock – Frome line
runs through the station site. Along the former alignment
runs a section of the National Cycle Network No 24. In
August 2010 access to the station site was possible along the
station approach road which was impossible on a previous
visit in 2002. In 2010 limited remains of the former station
could be seen; these included building foundations, a railway
gate and a section of old railings which ran behind the former
down (north) side platform.

MENDIP VALE   ST 638424

Opened: 1992
Closed: Remains open on the East Somerset Railway.
The 2010 western terminus of the restored East Somerset
Railway, the platform with a paving slab and gravel surface is
supported by concrete blocks. No shelter is provided on the
platform on the south side of the single track line.

MERRYFIELD LANE   ST 653425

Opened: 4.4.1980 with the commencement of services on
the restored East Somerset Railway from Cranmore.
Closed: Remains open on the East Somerset Railway.

The single platform with a wooden edge and gravel surface
stands on the down (south) side of the single track line on
the restored East Somerset Railway. At the platform's east
end is an iron shelter with a seat inside. A further seat is
provided on the platform.

MIDFORD   ST 761607

Opened: 20.7.1874 with the opening of the Bath Extension
of the Somerset & Dorset Railway, Evercreech Junction –
Bath.
Closed: Passengers: 7.3.1966 with closure of the Bristol –
Poole line to passenger services; Goods: 10.6.1963.
The derelict station building was demolished in December
1967 but the platform survived. In the mid 1980s
preservation attempts were undertaken, the platform being
cleared and resurfaced; the steps to the houses above
were also cleared. It was hoped that the station could be
developed as a heritage centre. A visit in September 2010
however revealed neglect with the platform overgrown and
the steps blocked.

The former trackbed alongside the platform has been
resurfaced and forms part of the National Cycle Network No
24. South of the station this route runs alongside the car park
of the 'Hope and Anchor' public house and over the surviving
splendid Midford viaduct towards Wellow. It is planned that
north of the station the route will link with the proposed Two
Tunnels shared path that is being developed through the
Combe Down and Devonshire Tunnels on the trackbed of the
Somerset & Dorset Railway into Bath.

MIDSOMER NORTON AND WELTON   ST 668548

Opened: 3.9.1873 with the opening of the Bristol & North
Somerset Railway, Bristol – Radstock. *Opened as Welton,
renamed Welton & Midsomer Norton on 2.5.1898 and
finally as Midsomer Norton & Welton 1.5.1904.*
Closed: Passengers: 2.11.1959 with closure of the Bristol –
Radstock – Frome line to passenger traffic; Goods: 15.6.1964.
Following final closure of the station in 1964, demolition
followed five years later in August 1969 after a fire. In 2010
only the eastern abutment of the high rail over bridge east
of the station site, the stone wall on the north side of the
former station approach road and the surviving Station Road
are specific reminders of railway activity. A new metal bridge
for cyclists and pedestrians using the surviving abutment has
been erected over Station Road carrying the National Cycle
Network No 48 which continues west through the former
station site.

MIDSOMER NORTON SOUTH   ST 664536

Opened: 20.7.1874 with the opening of the Bath Extension
of the Somerset & Dorset Railway, Evercreech Junction –
Bath. *Opened as Midsomer Norton, was renamed Midsomer
Norton & Wellow on 16.10.1898, Midsomer Norton Upper
on 26.9.1949 and Midsomer Norton South on 25.9.1950.*
Closed: Passengers: 7.3.1966 with closure of the Bath – Poole
line to passenger traffic; Goods: 15.6.1964.
Today the station site is the best surviving example of a

Somerset & Dorset Railway small station. In the 1990s some restoration was undertaken by an Avon County Council Youth Training Programme, which took over the task originally started as a youth project in the 1970s. Until 1995 the site was part of the Norton Radstock College Department of Art and Design. The site lease was then taken over by the Somerset & Dorset Railway Heritage Trust. Subsequently a great deal of restoration and development has taken place, very evident when the author visited the site in August 2010. The two platforms, former down (east) side main building and up side shelter are there, as is the former stone goods shed. The up side signal box, which had been demolished, is now rebuilt on the original stone base, the access steps and signal frame coming from Branksome station in Dorset (A signal lever in use was operated by the author!). At the time of the visit the greenhouse beside the signal box was being reconstructed, a restoration of a once familiar feature at the station. A quarter mile of track has been re-laid south towards Chilcompton, on which operations began on 11 September 2010. The goods shed is in use as a restoration workshop. Also on site is a picnic area with tables.

MILBORNE PORT   ST 675208
Opened: 7.5.1860 with the opening of the Gillingham – Sherborne section of the Salisbury & Yeovil Railway.
Closed: Passengers: 7.3.1966; Goods: 6.11.1961.
The surviving station building, including the station master's house, continues in residential use, 'The Station House'. Two pairs of former railway cottages sited behind each end of the up platform are also in residential use, 'Station Cottages' and '3/4 Station Cottages'. The former up (north) side platform remains, though somewhat overgrown.

MILTON ROAD HALT   ST 345621
Opened 1.12.1897 with the opening of the Weston – super-Mare – Clevedon section of the Weston, Clevedon & Portishead Light Railway.
Closed: 20.5.1940 with closure of the line.
No trace of the halt, at which an asbestos covered shelter but no platform was provided, can now be seen.

MILVERTON   ST 125262
Opened: 8.6.1871 with the opening of the Norton Junction – Wiveliscombe section of the Devon & Somerset Railway.
Closed: Passengers: 3.10.1966 with closure of the Norton Junction – Barnstaple line; Goods: 30.9.1963.
All trace of this station has gone with the trackbed running north-west from the site, taken over by the new alignment of the B3227 by-passing Milverton. Station Road running south into the village is the sole reminder of the railway era; of interest is that the flower beds at the B3227/Station Road junction are bordered by old wooden railway sleepers.

MINEHEAD   SS 975463
Opened: 16.7.1874 with the opening of the Minehead Railway, Watchet – Minehead.
Closed: Passengers: 4.1.1971 with closure of the Minehead branch, Norton Junction – Minehead; Goods: 6.7.1964.
Reopened: 28.3.1976 with the opening of the Minehead – Blue Anchor section of the restored West Somerset Railway. Since its reopening in 1976 considerable conversion and renovation has been undertaken on the now listed building. Its basic form is that following a major extension in the 1920s and further modifications in 1934, the latter including lengthening of the platform and the erection of a 200 ft long canopy. The former booking office, waiting and staff rooms have been converted into offices for the West Somerset Railway. These include an information office and an office for the WSR station master. The former parcels office is now the station shop, 'The Buffer Stop'. A new booking office has been added at the sea front end of the building incorporating fixtures brought from Cardiff General (now Central) Station. On the platform is an old drinking fountain; the lampposts are 1934 originals though the tops are reproductions.

When the WSR took over the station site in 1975 the goods shed opposite the station platform was converted into a locomotive depot and workshop; this included the digging of an engine inspection pit down the entire length of the shed. The former goods office at the town end was converted into a staff mess room. In 1997/98 a major extension was added on the east end of the shed. In 1991 a new carriage and wagon works building was constructed at the east end of the station on the sea side of the long platform. Most of the area originally occupied by the engine shed, the original turntable and part of the carriage sidings to the south of the station, was converted into use as a pay and display car park. A major recent project was the installation in 2007/08 of a large turntable adjacent to the station building, one of a number of items at the station originally at Pwllheli; before final installation it was extended to 65 ft to accommodate the large engines terminating at Minehead. Alongside is the new 'Turntable Café', opened in 2009. Adjoining the car park the original 'Railway Cottages' continue in residential use as 'Station Terrace'. The goods sidings on the landward side of the site, which once served several merchants and the cattle market, are now covered by the Mart Road Industrial Estate, including Travis Perkins.

In 1996 the Friends of Minehead Station was formed and has done much to improve the station facilities. This has included completion of the platform tarmacing, the installation of canopy lighting (originally from Taunton station) and also assistance with the renewal of the canopy itself, this costing some £275,000. This restoration was recognised in December 2005 when the WSR and contractors Bluestone jointly received the First Engineering Craft Skills Award for the high standard of work on the project.

MONKTON COMBE   ST 773619
Opened: 9.5.1910 with the opening of the Cam Valley line, Camerton – Limpley Stoke.
Closed: Passengers: 21.9.1925 with closure of the Hallatrow – Limpley Stoke line to passenger traffic; Goods: 15.2.1951.
Also temporary closures: Passengers: 22.3.1915 to 9.7.1923;

Goods: 1.4.1918 to 9.7.1928, originally as war time measures. Just as Camerton, along the Cam Valley line, had featured in the 1931 film, 'The Ghost Train', Monkton Combe was the location for filming 'The Titfield Thunderbolt' in 1952. The station was renovated and renamed Titfield. The canopy was extended and a new external ticket window constructed. The station was also provided with a number of period details such as weighing and chocolate machines but, when filming finished, all the extra details were removed and the station returned to its original state. It lasted another six years before demolition in 1958. The station site remained open but derelict for some years until the land was taken over and raised for Monkton Combe School's new all weather sports pitch in the late 1970s.

Today the only remains of the station are two black painted gateposts either side of a modern garage on the east side of Mill Lane. These were the gateposts of the road entrance. Close by stands 'No 1 Station Cottages'.

MONTACUTE   ST 497178

Opened: 27.1.1882 on the Durston – Yeovil Hendford branch from the Bristol & Exeter Railway, originally opened for passenger traffic on 1.10.1853.

Closed: Passengers: 15.6.1964 with closure of the Taunton – Yeovil line to passenger traffic; Goods: 30.9.1963.

The use of the trackbed for the new A3088 link road from Yeovil to the Cartgate roundabout on the A303 erased all trace of the station itself. Sections of the concrete platform, which had replaced the original timber construction, now form the platform at Doniford Beach Halt on the West Somerset Railway. However the station master's house above the east side of the A3088 survives in residential use, 'Station House'. There are remains of an old station entrance kissing gate adjacent to the house drive, close to the road.

NAILSEA AND BACKWELL   ST 479693

Opened: 14.6.1841 with the opening of the Bristol – Bridgwater section of the Bristol & Exeter Railway. *Opened as Nailsea, the suffix 'and Backwell' added 1.5.1905; reverted to Nailsea on 6.5.1974 but today is again known as Nailsea and Backwell.*

Closed: Passengers: Remains open, generally for local services on the Bristol – Taunton line, but also some peak hour services to and from London (Paddington); Goods: 1.7.1964. Major refurbishment was undertaken in the mid 1980s; the principal stone building on the up (towards Bristol) side had been demolished some years earlier but the down side wooden shelter with characteristic Bristol & Exeter bargeboards had survived. A 150 space car park was laid out which, when seen in September 2010, was full. The foundations of the original up side building can still be seen but modern shelters now serve passengers on both platforms, the early down side shelter now gone. Indication of the dominance of passengers travelling into Bristol is the presence of three metal and glass shelters on the up side, two being combined with a small hut that serves as a booking office. The refurbished 1907 open metal footbridge

manufactured by Finch & Co of Chepstow connects the platforms at the east end.

NIGHTINGALE VALLEY HALT   ST 563732

Opened: 9.7.1928 on the Portishead branch originally opened on 18.4.1867. Halt opened in summers only.

Closed: 12.9.1932.

Today no trace remains of this very short lived halt serving a local beauty spot in the Avon Gorge almost underneath the Clifton Suspension Bridge.

NORTON FITZWARREN   ST 195255

Opened: 2.6.1873 on the Taunton – Beam Bridge section of the Bristol & Exeter Railway originally opened on 1.5.1843.

Closed: Passengers: 30.10.1961; Goods: 6.7.1964.

Today it is hard to believe that this junction station ever existed. At the southern end of Station Road (the only remaining clue to the former extensive activity at the station) a tall wire fence runs alongside the West of England main line. The goods yard to the east of this road, occupied for some years by Taunton Cider, was, when seen in August 2010, in the early stages of development for housing, 'The Old Cider Works'. The former Railway Hotel at the end of the road close to the fence was at that time derelict, damaged by a fire on 15th January 2008. It has now been demolished.

NORTON FITZWARREN (WEST SOMERSET RAILWAY)

ST 192256

Opened: 8.2009

A new concrete platform erected by the West Somerset Railway for limited use, for instance at the annual steam fair in August and other special occasions on the Railway.

OLDFIELD PARK   ST 736645

Opened: 18.2.1929 on the Bristol – Bath section of the GWR Bristol – London line originally opened 31.8.1840.

Closed: remains open for local passenger services on the Bristol – Bath line.

During the 1970s the station's iron arc roofed shelters dating from its 1929 opening were replaced by bus stop type shelters. In 1988 the Friends of Oldfield Park Station campaigned for and obtained better services. On 18th February 1989 to celebrate the station's 60th Anniversary an art exhibition, attended by the author, was held at a nearby church hall. In 1994 the station was refurbished, new shelters being provided and long ramps installed to both platforms allowing disabled access. A small ticket office was installed at the foot of the down side ramp; on this side there are two shelters reflecting the dominance of passenger movement towards Bristol.

Today, under the 'Adopt a Station' scheme, the Oldfield Park Station Community Project tends the garden behind both platforms including the station name spelt out in white painted stones (a practice often found at stations many years ago). A mosaic, 'Oldfield Park', constructed by pupils at Hayesfield Girls School, is behind the down platform.

PAULTON HALT   ST 653576

Opened: 5.1.1914 on the Hallatrow – Camerton section of the Cam Valley line originally opened for passenger traffic on 1.4.1882.

Closed: 21.9.1925 with closure of the Hallatrow – Limpley Stoke line to passenger traffic.

Also temporary closure 22.3.1915 to 9.7.1923, originally as a war time measure.

When visiting the site in early September 2010 a small section of the platform's stone edge could possibly be seen alongside the former track alignment. The road over bridge north-east of the halt site was no longer evident. The access path to the halt and sections of old railway style fencing were apparent. A metal gate and steps down from a minor road, a section of the Limestone Link Trail, lead to the access path.

PENSFORD   ST 617639

Opened: 3.9.1873 with the opening of the Bristol & North Somerset Railway, Bristol – Radstock.

Closed: Passengers: 2.11.1959 with closure of the Bristol – Radstock – Frome line to passenger traffic; Goods: 15.6.1964. The whole station site has been developed for housing. 'Station House', the station master's house on Station Approach, continues in residential use, its design contrasting with the surrounding modern houses. A nearby reminder of the railway era at Pensford is the splendid surviving viaduct, south of the station, that carried the Bristol – Radstock line over the River Chew valley.

PILL   ST 525761

Opened: 18.4.1867 with the opening of the Portishead branch from the Bristol – Taunton line.

Closed: Passengers: 7.9.1964 with closure of the Portishead branch to passenger traffic; *Goods*: 10.6.1963.

Today sections of the two platforms, particularly on the up (towards Bristol) side, can be seen in the cutting north-west of the road over bridge. The relaid single line serving Royal Portbury Docks runs between them. The station master's house and booking office/waiting room remain above the platform beside the road bridge. When seen in August 2010, the booking office/waiting room was occupied by a building design firm and a baby supplies shop and the house section was in residential use.

POLSHAM HALT   ST 517429

Opened: 12.1861 on the Glastonbury – Wells branch of the Somerset Central Railway, originally opened on 15.3.1859

Closed: Passengers and Goods: 29.10.1951 with closure of the Glastonbury – Wells branch of the Somerset & Dorset Railway.

Some 60 years after closure the 1894 station building and the later 1920 station master's house remain in residential use. Two level crossing posts survive in the hedge at the south end of the station where the Wells branch crossed the minor road to Polsham village. Close by, in the garden beside the house, appears to be a surviving ground frame hut.

Also seen in 2010 were two further posts and a damaged gate across the former access to a small yard with a siding opposite the station.

PORTBURY   ST 497757

Opened: 18.4.1867 with the opening of the Portishead branch from the Bristol – Taunton line.

Closed: Passengers and Goods: 30.4.1962.

Today the impressive station building, incorporating accommodation for the station master, continues, with extensions, in residential use, 'Station House'. It is just east of the road bridge carrying the original alignment of the A369 Bristol to Portishead road (Station Road). A rusty single track, part of the original branch to Portishead, passes alongside the building and under the road bridge. It is largely hidden by thick undergrowth.

PORTBURY SHIPYARD   ST 509761

Opened: 16.9.1918 on the Portishead branch originally opened on 18.4.1867.

Closed: 26.3.1923.

Today there is no trace of this short lived facility developed at the end of the First World War to serve initially a proposed shipyard and then an Admiralty Office. Rusty track on the former Portishead branch passes through the site.

PORTISHEAD

First Station   ST 471769

Opened: 18.4.1867 with the opening of the Portishead branch from the Bristol – Taunton line.

Closed: 4.1.1954 with the redevelopment of the site, replaced by the 2nd station.

The site of the first station was taken over in the 1950s with the construction of the Portishead B Power Station. This is turn was demolished and the site is now covered by development south-east of Station Road that now leads to the new Marina housing development. The southern part of the station site is now used by Portishead Primary School.

Second Station   ST 469766

Opened: 4.1.1954 replacing the first station;

Closed: Passengers: 7.9.1964 with closure of the Portishead branch to passenger traffic; Goods: 1.5.1967.

Following closure in 1964, the station booking office and forecourt were incorporated into a petrol filling station, 'Station Garage', opening in October 1966. Some ten years ago the site was redeveloped, the station building being demolished. It is now a completely new structure, 'Waitrose Filling Station'.

PORTISHEAD (WCPLR)   ST 468764

Opened: 7.8.1907 as the northern terminus of the Clevedon – Portishead section of the Weston, Clevedon & Portishead Light Railway.

Closed: 20.5.1940 with closure of the line.

The site of the station, with a rustic style building, is now covered by the north-west section of Wyndham Way, close to the rear of the 'White Lion' public house. The line towards

Clevedon followed the approximate alignment of the road until it turned south past the east end of Albert Road.

PORTISHEAD SOUTH ST 469755
Opened: 7.8.1907 with the opening of the Clevedon – Portishead section of the Weston, Clevedon & Portishead Light Railway.
Closed: 20.5.1940.
No trace of this station, at which a wooden shelter but no platform was provided, can now be seen.

PUXTON AND WORLE ST 377630
Opened: 14.6.1841 with the opening of the Bristol – Bridgwater section of the Bristol & Exeter Railway. *Opened as Banwell, renamed Worle 3.8.1869, renamed Puxton 1.3.1884 and finally Puxton and Worle 1.3.1922.*
Closed: Passengers: 6.4.1964; Goods: 10.6.1963.
Apart from short lengths of railings and gates, no trace of this station survives at trackside. The station master's house at the east end of the site on the down (towards Taunton) side continues in residential use, 'Station House'. At the junction of Bourton Lane and Station Road, a large signal box at the west end of the station site beyond the level crossing on the Bristol to Taunton line, survives as a crossing box. New windows have been installed in the box.

PYLLE ST 618388
Opened: 3.2.1862 with the opening of the Glastonbury – Cole section of the Somerset Central Railway.
Closed: Passengers: 7.3.1966 with closure of the Evercreech Junction to Highbridge line to passenger traffic; Goods: 10.6.1963.
Following closure of the station in 1966 the goods shed with an extension partly over the trackbed was used as a meat packing plant. A period of disuse followed until the shed was redeveloped in the late 1980s as a large house, 'Pylle Halt'. The station master's house, attached unusually to the eastern end of the goods shed, also continues in residential use, 'Station House'. The station building on the south side of the line has also been converted into a house with an extension and new structures both behind and to the east. Some sections of the up (south) platform remain. To the east of this housing group the former A37 over bridge has been replaced by an embankment.

RADFORD AND TIMSBURY HALT ST 672579
Opened: 9.5.1910 with the opening of the Cam Valley line, Camerton – Limpley Stoke.
Closed: 21.8.1925 with closure of the Hallatrow – Limpley Stoke line to passenger traffic.
Also temporary closure 22.3.1915 to 9.7.1923, originally as a war time measure.
Today a public footpath (part of the Limestone Link) runs from Radford Hill through the site at which no trace of the halt now remains. Alongside the footpath isolated sections of rail track act as posts. A stone wall remains in place along the north of the former site of the halt.

RADSTOCK NORTH ST 689550
Opened: 20.7.1874 with the opening of the Bath Extension of the Somerset & Dorset Railway Evercreech Junction – Bath. *The suffix 'North' added formally 26.9.1949.*
Closed: Passengers: 7.3.1966 with closure of the Bath – Poole line to passenger traffic; Goods: 15.6.1964.
The site of the station, whose buildings were demolished in the late 1970s, has been redeveloped with a car park at the east end and a landscaped area with flower beds and seating at the west end. In the latter there was originally a large winding wheel from one of the local collieries but this has now been replaced by a tall structure surmounted by a smaller wheel. The goods yard, east of the station, has been redeveloped for housing including road access via Pines Way and Pine Court (the latter without an 's'!), a reminder that the Pines Express from Manchester to Bournemouth once ran through the station.

RADSTOCK WEST ST 689549
Opened: 3.9.1873 with the opening of the Bristol & North Somerset Railway, Bristol – Radstock. *The suffix 'West' added formally 26.9.1949.*
Closed: Passengers: 2.11.1959 with closure of the Bristol – Radstock – Frome line to passenger traffic; Goods: 29.11.1965.
The main station building and platform on the up (south) side were demolished in 1963, the site being redeveloped for shopping units on Fortescue Road. The double track through the site survived for some years as did the shelter on the former down platform. When viewed in 2002 the derelict down platform was the only visible remnant but, when re-visited in 2010, this could not be seen in dense undergrowth behind a notice for the Norton Radstock Regeneration Company. On the road south-west from the station site (Wells Road) is 'The Railway' public house.

ROADWATER ST 032382
Opened: 4.9.1865 with the introduction of passenger services on the West Somerset Mineral Railway, Comberow – Watchet.
Closed: 8.11.1898 with the withdrawal of passenger services on the line. Also a temporary limited revival of passenger services 1907-1910.
Today the station building with extensions survives as a house in the village. A section of platform is also still there in the garden laid out partly over the former trackbed. South of the station an old level crossing gate survives as do girders which formed part of a bridge that carried the mineral line over a stream. South of this point the trackbed has been converted into a road; a sign states 'The Mineral Line'.

SALTFORD ST 688669
Opened: 16.12.1840 on the Bristol – Bath section of the GWR Bristol – London line, opened some four months earlier on 31.8.1840.
Closed: Passengers: 5.1.1970; Goods: 1.9.1959.

In 2010 the station buildings and platforms have entirely gone. Much of the station site on the down (south) side is used by Network Rail as a depot, 'Saltford Yard', in particular for storage of materials such as new concrete sleepers. A section of railway style railings survives alongside the depot access from the A4 road between Bristol and Bath.

SANDFORD AND BANWELL   ST 416596
Opened: 3.8.1869 with the opening of the Yatton – Cheddar section of the Cheddar Valley & Yatton Railway. *The suffix 'and Banwell' added soon after opening.*
Closed: Passengers: 9.9.1963 with closure of the Yatton – Witham line to passenger traffic; Goods: 10.6.1963.
Following closure of the station in 1963, the buildings remained largely intact and in the late 1970s the site was occupied by 'Sandford Stone', the station building, goods shed and station master's house all being retained and used.

In 2008 the whole site, together with an adjacent farm, was taken over and developed as a 93 unit retirement village by St Monica's Trust, a Bristol based organisation. Appropriately named 'Sandford Station' the complex includes, in addition to many new housing units, the magnificently restored station building and platform (with a section of track and two trucks sited by the platform), the former goods shed (converted into the Pullman Restaurant) and the former station master's house (restored as a three bedroom house). The goods shed office is now the office for the restaurant chef. Inside the restaurant signs are in a GWR style and colour and the walls are adorned with railway posters and photographs. Overall the site is, without doubt, one of the best examples of a restored station complex, not only in Somerset but in the South West, with all the station facilities renovated and reused.

SHAPWICK   ST 423412
Opened: 28.8.1854 with the opening of the Highbridge Wharf – Glastonbury section of the Somerset Central Railway.
Closed: Passengers: 7.3.1966 with closure of the Evercreech Junction – Highbridge line to passenger traffic; Goods: 10.6.1963.
Sited where Station Road, running north from the village of Shapwick, reaches South Drain, there is now virtually no evidence remaining of the station, the only visible element being a solitary concrete post at the entrance to the former goods yard on the east side of the road south of the Drain. Station Farm is a little to the north on Shapwick Road and all around are piles of peat, remnants of an activity that once provided much business to the station. The 1861 station master's/signalman's house north of the station on the east side of Shapwick Road has long been demolished.

SHEPTON MALLET CHARLTON ROAD   ST 629430
Opened: 20.7.1874 with the opening of the Bath Extension of the Somerset & Dorset Railway, Evercreech Junction – Bath. *The suffix 'Charlton Road' was used from October 1883.*

Closed: Passengers: 7.3.1966 with closure of the Bath – Poole line to passenger traffic; Goods: 10.6.1963.
The station buildings were demolished and the site cleared for redevelopment over the period 1970-1972. The site, now Crowne Trading Estate, is used by a range of industrial and commercial firms, in particular a large haulage contractor. There is very little evidence that the station and railway ever existed, the exceptions are an end of the former railway embankment on the north side of Charlton Road and the station master's house on the south side of the road east of the station, 'Station House'.

SHEPTON MALLET HIGH STREET   ST 618432
Opened: 9.11.1858 with the opening of the Witham – Shepton Mallet section of the East Somerset Railway. *The suffix 'High Street' added 26.9.1949.*
Closed: Passengers: 9.9.1963 with closure of the Yatton – Witham line to passenger traffic; Goods: 13.7.1964.
Today the situation varies over the former station site, located to the east of the recent retail park, dominated by the new Tesco store. The eastern end of the site is derelict and the main station building, which was in use in 2002 by a cleaning supplies firm, has now gone. At the western end the goods shed is still there with a number of extensions including a modern office block, occupied by a restoration and building firm.

SHOSCOMBE AND SINGLE HILL HALT   ST 720562
Opened: 23.9.1929 on the Bath Extension of the Somerset & Dorset Railway originally opened on 20.7.1874.
Closed: 7.3.1966 with closure of the Bath – Poole line to passenger traffic.
The halt has completely gone but the abutments of the road over bridge just to the east of the station site are a clear indication of where the Somerset & Dorset line between Bath and Radstock passed through the valley. An isolated iron post, now covered in ivy at the road side at the base of the embankment, marks the original road side entrance to the path leading up to the south side platform.

SOMERTON (SOMERSET)   ST 486285
Opened: 2.7.1906 on the Curry Rivel Junction – Somerton section of the GWR cut off route, Castle Cary – Cogload Junction opened originally for goods traffic to and from the west on 12.2.1906. *The suffix 'Somerset' was to avoid confusion with the station of the same name in Oxfordshire.*
Closed: Passengers: 10.9.1962 with the withdrawal of local passenger services Castle Cary - Taunton; Goods: 6.7.1964.
Today no line side trace remains of the station, formerly sited in the deep cutting in the centre of Somerton and south-west of a high road over bridge at the west end of West Street. On Station Path, the former access to the down (south-east) platform, and also in the vicinity of the road bridge, are sections of railway style railings, posts and gates. On Station Path itself a house garage, built in the style of a goods shed, has on its wall an old metal notice, 'Beware of Trains'. The former goods yard and cattle market on the

up (north-west) side have been redeveloped for housing accessed by Great Western Lane. In the town centre are the Brunel Precinct and Brunel Close.

SPARKFORD   ST 606265

Opened 1.9.1856 with the opening of the Frome – Yeovil section of the Wilts, Somerset & Weymouth Railway.
Closed: Passengers: 3.10.1966; Goods: 7.1.1963.
No remains of the station survive. The line, singled in May 1968, is now crossed north of the station site by the concrete bridge of the A303 Sparkford by-pass. South-west of the station, the former large creamery building, at one time rail served, is now occupied by Haynes Publishing, famous for its car manuals.

STOGUMBER   ST 110372

Opened: 31.3.1862 with the opening of the West Somerset Railway, Norton Junction – Watchet.
Closed: Passengers: 4.1.1971 with closure of the Minehead branch, Norton Junction – Minehead; Goods: 19.8.1963.
Reopened: 7.5.1978 with the opening of the Williton – Stogumber section of the restored West Somerset Railway. The smallest station on the reopened West Somerset Railway has an unusual layout with the main station building at ground level on the up (towards Bishops Lydeard) side and the raised platform on the down. The 1862 building has recently undergone refurbishment including a complete renewal of the floor and the installation of a kitchen unit to provide refreshments for passengers and passing visitors. Improvements have been undertaken with the support of the Friends of Stogumber Station (FOSS). The large goods shed north of the building was demolished in 1963 with the site now laid out as an attractive picnic area, including a roofed picnic table in memory of Harry Horn, who was station master for many years until his death in 2000 aged 96. The former cattle dock south of the building can still be identified, the only one on the WSR almost intact, the remainder being demolished.

The original platform on the west side of the single line was principally constructed of wood but this has been rebuilt with concrete supports under a tarmac and paving slab surface. Period style lampposts have been erected on the platform, on the former station building and in the adjoining small car park. One of these came from St Ives in Cornwall. A new small passenger shelter, made by local craftsmen was erected in 1992 on the north end of the platform. An early GWR shelter on the south end was demolished in 2008 and, when the author visited in July 2010, the replacement shelter, in a similar style but with a store underneath, was nearing completion. Its official opening took place on 15 May 2011. The station master's house high above the station on the up side continues in residential use; in mid 2010 it was up for auction with a guide price of £225,000. The former 'Railway Hotel' below the station on the down side also remains, now in residential use.

STRAP LANE HALT   ST 724387

Opened: 18.7.1932 on the Frome – Castle Cary line originally opened 1.9.1856.
Closed: 5.6.1950
Also temporary closure 6.10.1941 to 16.12.1946 as a war time measure.
Closed over 60 years ago, no trace of the halt remains at trackside. A July 2010 visit found isolated posts in undergrowth on either side of the adjacent road over bridge that probably stood alongside access steps to the two timber platforms.

SUTTON BINGHAM   ST 549115

Opened: 19.7.1860 with the opening of the Yeovil Junction – Exeter section of the London & South Western Railway.
Closed: Passengers: 31.12.1962; Goods: 4.4.1960.
Today only a small section of the former up (north) side platform can be seen. East of the former station adjacent to the site of the goods yard two former railway cottages continue in residential use, nos '1 and 2 Railway Cottages'.

TAUNTON   ST 227254

Opened: 1.7.1842 with the opening of the Bridgwater – Taunton section of the Bristol & Exeter Railway.
Closed: Passengers: remains open with inter-city services to and from London (Paddington), the Midlands, the North and the West Country and also local services on the Bristol – Exeter line; Goods:1963 (local yards) 1972 (Freight Concentration Depot).
The layout of Taunton station in 2010 is basically that which resulted from major changes between 1930 and 1932 when the number of through tracks between Cogload Junction to the east of Taunton and Norton Fitzwarren to the west was changed from two to four. The 1878 overall roof was demolished and a revised layout of four through platform faces (two on an island platform) and five bay platforms was brought into use. The early buildings on the down (towards Exeter) side, including an original 1842 block, were retained but major rebuilding took place on the up side including a new entrance and booking office at the north-east end of a new subway which came into use in January 1932. Passenger traffic at Taunton dwindled in the 1960s, particularly with the withdrawal of services on all the branch lines focusing on the station. The two faces of the island platform were taken out of use in March 1967, the two central lines being then used only by through passenger and freight trains. The building and canopies were removed and replaced on the retained platform by trees and advertisement hoardings. Use of a number of the bay platforms also ceased.

On 16th March 1983 a new booking office and travel centre was opened on the north side. A major change came in 2000 with the re-instatement of the island platform for use by both inter-city and local trains. The old entrance from the subway was renovated and a new platform shelter erected. Once again Taunton station has four through platform faces in use, together with a bay at the north end of the up platform, used occasionally for local trains in the Bristol direction.

The former Great Western Hotel, to the rear of the down side buildings, is now offices named 'Great Western House'. The white lettering 'British Railways Taunton Freight Concentration Depot' on a derelict building on the down side, east of the station, is a relic of times past, having closed in 1972. A large area of former railway land on the down side to the north of the station was, in late 2010, being redeveloped for housing (106 apartments). A surviving shed was advertised as being to let.

TEMPLECOMBE LOWER   ST 710228

Opened: 3.2.1862 with the opening of the Cole – Templecombe section of the Dorset Central Railway.
Closed: 17.1.1887 following diversion of most Somerset & Dorset Railway through passenger trains to Templecombe Upper on the Salisbury – Yeovil line.
Today there is no trace of the station nearly 125 years after its closure.

TEMPLECOMBE LOWER PLATFORM   ST 711227

Opened: 17.1.1887 replacing the earlier Templecombe Lower station which was a little to the north.
Closed: 3.1.1966.
This simple platform served the limited number of through trains on the Somerset & Dorset Railway not calling at Templecombe Upper station, thus avoiding reversal of the trains. Today there is no trace of this little used platform.

TEMPLECOMBE UPPER   ST 708226

Opened: 7.5.1860 with the opening of the Gillingham – Sherborne section of the Salisbury & Yeovil Railway.
Closed: Passengers: 7.3.1966 with closure of the Bath – Poole line to passenger traffic; Goods: 5.4.1965.
Reopened: 3.10.1983 (see below) now with regular passenger services on the London (Waterloo), Salisbury and Exeter line.
In 1968, although a 1938 signal box was retained, the main station buildings, rebuilt in the 1930s, were demolished and much of the Salisbury to Exeter line was reduced to single track. This was not the end for Templecombe station – thanks largely to the sterling efforts of the Templecombe Station Working Committee (TSWC). After early difficulties, British Rail agreed to stop a train at Templecombe once again, using the former up platform. Building on initial success the TSWC organised a number of excursions from Templecombe, also undertaking a large amount of voluntary work at the station to meet the requirements of British Rail. This included the provision of lighting. The excursions were a great success and the Committee earned the respect of the County Council and British Rail. Eventually, after extensive work had been undertaken by the Committee, the station reopened on 3rd October 1983, initially for a three year experiment, half the upper floor of the signal box doubling as a booking office. In 1988 a small platform shelter was built; this was added to in 1990 by the construction of a new

building with toilets and other facilities. An 1893 footbridge was also erected, transferred from the station at Buxted in East Sussex. When seen in July 2010 it was in need of a new coat of paint and rust was evident.

Through the 1990s business continued to flourish. In the 1980s and 1990s the station itself, through support of volunteers from the Templecombe Station Promotion Group won many local and national awards. Flower beds and a lawn continue to enhance the station. On the lawn stands a stone sun dial sculpture erected in 1990, commissioned by the British Rail Community Unit. The figure is holding a stone passenger timetable. Sadly when seen in 2010 the stone was flaking and the sculpture was in need of attention. Opposite the junction of Station Road and High Street is the 'Royal Wessex' public house, an inappropriate name as this train ran on the Waterloo to Weymouth line!

THORNEY AND KINGSBURY HALT   ST 427232

Opened: 28.11.1927 on the Durston – Yeovil line originally opened for passenger traffic on 1.10.1863.
Closed: 15.6.1964 with closure of the Taunton – Yeovil line to passenger traffic.
When previously viewed in 2002 a small section of the concrete platform could be seen from the adjoining road over bridge. Viewed again in July 2010, nothing could be seen in a vast area of brambles. However a small section of railway fencing could be seen at the roadside at the north end of the bridge.

THORNFALCON   ST 274240

Opened 1.3.1870 on the Taunton – Chard branch from the Bristol & Exeter Railway originally opened on 11.9.1866.
Opened as Thorne Falcon, changed to Thorne until 7.1890 and then to Thornfalcon from 1.1.1902.
Closed: 6.7.1964 with closure of the Taunton – Chard Junction line to passenger traffic.
Also temporary closure to all traffic 5.2.1951 to 7.5.1951 due to fuel crisis.
Most of the station site has been taken over by the northern end of the recent dual carriageway section of the A358 between Henlade and Ash Cross. Small sections of railings possibly associated with the railway can be seen but there is no trace of the station structures.

TWERTON-ON-AVON   ST 729647

Opened: 16.12.1840 on the Bristol – Bath section of the GWR Bristol – London line originally opened on 31.8.1840.
Closed: 2.4.1917 as a war time economy but never reopened.
The platform was removed soon after closure but the main station building on the up (towards Bath) side remained on the Lower Bristol Road. In the mid 1960s it was used by a heating and plumbing firm and subsequently by a retail unit selling garden ornaments. When seen in May 2010, the Grade II listed building was unused and early in 2011 scaffolding was erected around the building.

VENN CROSS   ST 033246

Opened: 1.11.1873 with the opening of the Wiveliscombe – Barnstaple section of the Devon & Somerset Railway.

Closed: Passengers: 3.10.1966 with closure of the Norton Junction – Barnstaple line; Goods: 30.9.1963.

Today the combined station master's house and station building are in residential use, the former named 'Station House' and the latter 'Booking Office'. The deep cutting north of the building is now a garden. A section of old railings surviveS alongside a short cul-de-sac serving the houses on the north side of the B3227, created following a road realignment. West of the former platform in the cutting and just sited in Devon the former goods shed has been converted into a large house named inaccurately 'The Engine House'. Further west an old distant signal stands in a field beside the former trackbed.

WALTON-IN-GORDANO HALT   ST 428731

Opened: 7.8.1907 with the opening of the Clevedon – Portishead section of the Weston, Clevedon & Portishead Light Railway.

Closed: 20.5.1940 with closure of the line.

No trace of this halt, at which there was a wooden shelter but no platform, can now be seen.

WALTON PARK HALT   ST 418724

Opened: 7.8.1907 with the opening of the Clevedon – Portishead section of the Weston, Clevedon & Portishead Light Railway.

Closed: 20.5.1940 with closure of the line.

No trace of this halt, at which a rustic style hut but no platform was provided, can now be seen.

WANSTROW   ST 711413

Opened: 1.1.1860 on the Witham – Shepton Mallet section of the East Somerset Railway originally opened on 9.11.1858.

Closed: Passengers: 9.9.1963 with closure of the Yatton – Witham line to passenger traffic; Goods: 10.6.1963.

Today no trace of the station remains at trackside on the single line that remains open for freight trains to Merehead Quarry and which also gives rail access to the East Somerset Railway at Cranmore. A path originally led to the station from south of the rail bridge over the A359 that runs north as Station Road to Wanstrow village. Broken remains of the entrance gate to the path at the road side were visible in July 2010 but the line of the path was completely overgrown.

WASHFORD   ST 044412

Opened: 16.7.1874 with the opening of the Minehead Railway, Minehead – Watchet.

Closed: Passengers: 4.1.1971 with closure of the Minehead branch, Norton Junction – Minehead; Goods: 6.7.1974.

Reopened: 28.8.1976 with the opening of the Blue Anchor – Watchet section of the restored West Somerset Railway.

When the West Somerset Railway (WSR) was reopened through Washford in 1976 the station was leased to the Somerset & Dorset Railway Trust which, over the years,

has transformed the site. The main station building on the down platform has been carefully restored and fitted out in a Somerset & Dorset (S&D) style with artefacts from former S&D stations. It is the principal museum for the Trust with archives stored there. The small signal cabin at the east end of the down platform has been restored and fitted out in the manner of Midford box on the S&D line south of Bath.

The goods yard has been redeveloped to reflect the S&D era. The old goods shed had been demolished in 1964 and the sidings were lifted when the station closed. Track from Radstock and the Royal Ordnance Factory at Puriton near Bridgwater has been re-laid. A new large building at the west end of the goods yard was erected in 1988 and used as a restoration workshop. The main doors are from the S&D goods shed at Wells Priory Road and the main wall incorporates a cast iron window from the bonded store at Bath Green Park. Another artefact from the old Wells S&D goods shed is the wooden office building which is now sited at the Minehead end of the workshop. Donated to the Trust by the Wells Estates in 1988, it now contains models related to the S&D including a fine diorama of Highbridge Station.

Sited from 1989 in the goods yard at the east end is the small signal box from Burnham-on-Sea purchased by the Trust from the Toddington base of the Gloucestershire Warwickshire Railway (see Burnham-on-Sea text). It contains a display of signalling equipment. A visitor centre, commissioned in 1993, is sited in the body of a former London & North Western Railway Carriage Truck. The gates at the Minehead end of the S&D yard across the link to the WSR line are the former level crossing gates from Edington Burtle (Junction) on the S&D line east of Highbridge. The adjacent 'Washford Inn', the former Railway Hotel, has a fine sign showing an engine and carriages.

WASHFORD (WSMR)   ST 046411

Opened: 4.9.1865 with the introduction of passenger services on the West Somerset Mineral Railway, Comberow – Watchet.

Closed: 8.11.1898 with the withdrawal of passenger services on the line. Also a temporary limited revival of passenger services 1907 to 1910.

A modern bungalow stands on the site of the station which was between Lower Washford level crossing and the bridge carrying the main Williton to Minehead road over the West Somerset Mineral Railway.

WATCHET   ST 072433

Opened: 31.3.1862 as the terminus of the West Somerset Railway, Norton Junction – Watchet.

Closed: Passengers: 4.1.1971 with closure of the Minehead branch, Norton Junction – Minehead.

Reopened: 28.8.1976 with the opening of the Blue Anchor – Williton section of the restored West Somerset Railway.

The station's function as the terminus of the original 1862 West Somerset Railway from the main GWR line at Norton Junction, west of Taunton, explains why the main building was constructed at right angles to the line. Now renovated, it is used as a booking office and shop on the restored West Somerset Railway.

Also on the single platform is a 1907 GWR pagoda style shelter; for many years it was disused but, following restoration in 2006, it is now used as a visitor centre and waiting room, 'The Pagoda Waiting Room'. It contains displays setting out the input of Brunel to the West Somerset Railway, together with the history of the station and its surroundings. This was part of the WSR's tribute to Brunel in what was the 200th anniversary of his birth. Between the shelter and the main building the former store and lamp hut is now a garden shed used in the tending of the station's fine flower beds.

Beyond the pagoda hut is the Jubilee Geological Wall. Developed in 2004 on the foundations of the 1870s signal box, it includes examples of the many rocks found in the area. Following closure in 1971, the goods shed was the only one on the Minehead branch to be sold and is now the Watchet Boat Museum. The iron footbridge at the south-west end of the platform was also sold, in this case to the West Somerset District Council. When seen in July 2010 it was closed, being declared a dangerous structure and was removed in January 2011 for refurbishment.

WATCHET (WSMR) ST 070434

Opened: 4.9.1865 with the introduction of passenger services on the West Somerset Mineral Railway.
Closed: 8.11.1898 with the withdrawal of passenger services on the line. Also a temporary limited revival of passenger services 1907 - 1910.
The station site, closed to passengers over 100 years ago, is now a yard a short way inland from the West Pier to which mineral trains ran through the station. The two storey station house, with a date on the wall of 1855, survives as two flats, 'Old Station House', as does the stone goods shed, now a workshop, and another wooden shed now the 'Spice House Restaurant'. The original station platform and back wall are now enclosed on the east side of the yard behind the tall station house.

WELLINGTON ST 130212

Opened: 1.5.1843 with the opening of the Taunton – Beam Bridge section of the Bristol & Exeter Railway.
Closed: Passengers: 5.10.1964; Goods: 6.7.1964.
The original station was rebuilt in 1931/32 when the tracks through the site were quadrupled. Following closure in 1964, these later buildings were mostly demolished, the principal survivor being the original goods shed on the down (towards Exeter) side, adjacent to a road over bridge carrying the B3157 towards Milverton. When viewed in July 2010 limited remains of the 1930s down platform were visible but a loop line alongside, which was there, but disused in 2002, had gone. The large brick goods shed is now attached to a large concrete structure in the Swallowfield development, which occupies the former station site on the down side, both north and south of the road bridge. The road from the bridge running south-east towards the town centre is Station Road.

WELLOW ST 738581

Opened: 20.7.1874 with the opening of the Bath Extension of the Somerset & Dorset Railway, Evercreech Junction – Bath.
Closed: Passengers: 7.3.1966 with closure of the Bath – Poole line to passenger services; Goods: 10.6.1963.
Following closure, the station building was converted and extended to form a large house at the end of Station Road. When first converted it featured in a Living Homes magazine article on the conversion of former stations into dwellings. The main features of the building were retained including the canopy. A later extension at the south-west is an attractive feature. Rising above one of the chimneys is a weather vane in the form of an engine and tender. An attractive garden has been created on the former trackbed with both platforms visible.

The former goods yard to the south-west of the station is now a public car park. A little to the north-east of the station the former signal box is now, together with an adjacent new structure, in use as a dwelling, accessed by Railway Lane. Beyond the box the former station master's house continues as a dwelling, 'Station House', high above Mill Hill adjacent to abutments of a former high road over bridge.

WELLS EAST SOMERSET ST 546451

Opened: 1.3.1862 as the terminus of the Shepton Mallet – Wells section of the East Somerset Railway.
Closed: Passengers: 1.1.1878 with the start of through running of passenger trains between the Cheddar Valley and East Somerset Railways by-passing the station; Goods: 13.7.1964. Freight trains, mostly carrying stone, continued to pass the site until 29.4.1969.
Today there is no trace of the East Somerset station except for a small section of stone wall close to the former Railway Inn, now the 'Sherston Inn'. A stone plinth marks the former site of the station alongside East Somerset Way which follows the trackbed of the former East Somerset Railway between Wells and Witham. The plinth, one of three marking the sites of the three stations in the town has two metal plaques stating 'The Railway Age in Wells 1859 – 1969' and 'Wells (East Somerset)'.

WELLS PRIORY ROAD ST 545452

Opened: 15.3.1859 with the opening of the Glastonbury – Wells branch of the Somerset Central Railway. *The suffix 'Priory Road' was added in October 1883.*
Closed: Passengers: 29.10.1951 with closure of the Glastonbury – Wells line; Goods: 12.10.1964. Freight trains, mostly carrying stone, continued to pass through until 29.4.1969.
Soon after closure of the station to passengers in 1951 the train shed roof was removed. Subsequently the building itself was demolished. The stone goods shed was demolished in 1988, the material being used in the construction of a new building for the East Somerset Railway at Cranmore (see Cranmore text). The attached wooden office has been re-erected by the Somerset & Dorset Railway Trust

at its Washford site. Also relocated to Washford were the main doors of the goods shed (see Washford text). Today the Wells Priory Road station site and goods yard has been redeveloped and used by Travis Perkins, the builders' merchants and a Lidl supermarket. A stone plinth marks the former site of the station alongside the appropriately named Strawberry Way, which follows the former trackbed of the Yatton to Wells line, known affectionately as the 'Strawberry Line'. The plinth, one of three marking the sites of the three Wells stations, has two metal plaques stating 'The Railway Age in Wells 1859–1969' and 'Wells (Priory Road)'. The station master's house on the west side of Priory Road was demolished in 1995 during the layout of a new roundabout at the junction of Priory Road and the Wells Relief Road (East Somerset Way/Strawberry Way).

WELLS TUCKER STREET   ST 543457

Opened: 5.4.1870 with the opening of the Cheddar – Wells section of the Cheddar Valley & Yatton Railway. *The suffix 'Tucker Street' was added from 12.7.1920 but dropped from 6.5.1950.*
Closed: Passengers: 9.9.1963 with closure of the Yatton – Witham line to passenger traffic; Goods: 13.7.1964. Freight trains, mostly carrying stone, continued to pass through until 29.4.1969.
The station buildings and platforms have gone, much of the former site being now covered by the section of the Wells Ring Road known as Strawberry Way, reflecting the affectionate name of the former railway, 'Strawberry Line'. Behind the east side of the site the former Railway Cottages, built by the Bristol & Exeter Railway for its staff, remain, now called 'Cheddar Valley Buildings'.

The stone goods shed, north of the station and Tucker Street is the only significant ex railway structure still surviving, not only at Tucker Street but in Wells. In mid 2010 it was occupied by Roman Glass, Pine Plus and the Westfield Veterinary Centre. One of the entrances to the building erroneously states 'Old Engine Shed' as there was no such facility at Tucker Street station. A stone plinth, one of three marking the former sites of the three stations in Wells is on the east side of Strawberry Way. Two plaques on the plinth state 'The Railway Age in Wells 1859-1969' and 'Wells (Tucker Street)'. The nearby 'Cheddar Valley Inn' on Tucker Street at one time displayed a sign showing a train at Cheddar station but this was absent when seen in May 2010.

WESTON (BATH)   ST 731649

Opened: 4.8.1869 with the opening of the Mangotsfield – Bath branch from the Bristol – Gloucester line. *Opened as Weston, renamed Weston (Bath) from 1.10.1934.*
Closed: Passengers: 21.9.1953; Goods: 29.11.1965
Today the station building, on the north side of the former Mangotsfield to Bath line survives, primarily in use by the local radio station, Bath Fm. With a west end extension, it is in good condition with the railway style barge boards prominent. The former station master's house to the west of the station at the junction of Ashley Avenue and Station

Road continues in residential use with a rear extension (no 16 Station Road). Immediately to the south of the house two metal posts, originally part of the level crossing across Station Road, remain, though in May 2010 almost hidden in undergrowth. South of the station building and the station house the former trackbed is today covered in vegetation, trees and undergrowth. West of Station Road the former trackbed is a walkway. The trackbed through Weston station was, in 2010, identified as a potential route for a Bath Rapid Transit route from the west of the city to Bath city centre.

WESTON JUNCTION   ST 339603

Opened: 14.6.1841 with the opening of the Weston-super-Mare spur line and the Bristol – Bridgwater section of the Bristol & Exeter Railway.
Closed: 1.3.1884 with closure of the spur line replaced by the new loop line to the resort.
No trace of the station, closed over 125 years ago, now remains alongside the main Bristol – Taunton line that, in this section, by-passes the resort.

WESTON MILTON   ST 344614

Opened: 3.7.1933 on the Weston-super-Mare loop line originally opened on 1st March 1884. *Opened with the suffix 'Halt', this was dropped as from 5th May 1969.*
Closed: remains open principally for trains on the Taunton – Weston-super-Mare – Bristol services. Also limited peak hour services to and from London (Paddington).
This small station on the Weston-super-Mare loop line serves the eastern suburbs of the resort. With singling of this section of the loop line in 1972 the redundant concrete down (towards WsM) platform was transferred to the new Lympstone Commando station on the Exmouth branch in Devon. In 1983 the station was refurbished, a brick shelter being erected on the remaining platform. An enlarged car park for about forty cars was also laid out behind the platform; however, when visited in late September 2010 only six cars were parked. A plaque adjacent to the steps up to the platform from the car park indicates that artwork and flower beds at the station had been created by the pupils of Worle Community School, Westhaven School and Milton Park Primary School, funded by Network Rail, First Great Western, the Severnside Community Rail Partnership and North Somerset Council.

WESTON-SUPER-MARE
First Station   ST 321614

Opened: 14.6.1841 as the terminus of the Weston-super-Mare spur line from the Bristol – Bridgwater section of the Bristol & Exeter Railway that opened on the same day.
Closed: 20.7.1866 replaced by the second larger station on a slightly shortened spur line.
The station site at the west end of Alexandra Parade is today occupied by gardens and the floral clock. An information board in front of a replica engine erected in 2006 to

celebrate the 200th anniversary of Brunel's birth sets out the history of the first station.

Second Station ST 323613

Opened: 20.7.1866 as the replacement second terminus of the Weston-super-Mare spur line from the Bristol & Exeter Railway.

Closed: Passengers: 1.3.1884 with closure of the spur line and the opening of the loop line and the third station; Goods: 20.6.1966.

For a time after its closure in 1884 this 1866 station was used for band concerts, before being converted into a goods depot in 1900/01. It suffered bomb damage in June 1942 but remained in use until June 1966 when goods facilities were withdrawn from the town. It was finally demolished in 1984 to be replaced by the Tesco supermarket and Hildesheim Court residential development, though some of the structure had been removed in 1977. Short sections of the 1866 walls survive today on Station Road and Locking Road alongside the Tesco store.

Third Station ST 324611

Opened: 1.3.1884 with the opening of the Weston-super-Mare loop line replacing the spur line.

Closed: Passengers: remains open with good levels of local services on the Bristol – Taunton – Exeter line and some inter-city services to and from London (Paddington), the Midlands, the North and the West Country; Goods: 20.6.1966 (at site of second station). *Known at its opening as Weston-super-Mare General, it lost the suffix from 21.9.1953. It regained it from 6.5.1958 but it was dropped from 6.9.1964 when the Locking Road excursion station closed.*

The station today is basically as that completed in 1884 on the loop line. In 1986 it underwent a major face-lift and in 1994 extensive work was completed on the glazed canopy roofs. This followed a time when the future of this historic station building had seemed in doubt, the plan being to replace it with a new station on the main line by-passing the town. Much of the canopy iron work and glazing was replaced by modern materials, but retaining the original basic ridge and furrow design.

The main offices continue today on the up platform with a modernised booking office, a bar/café 'Off the Rails', and a waiting room. The up side bay platform is no longer in use though the track remains, used for storage of rolling stock. No facilities are provided in the retained buildings on the down platform. The operation of the station is handicapped to some degree by the loop line; apart from through the station itself it is only single track, having been singled by 1972. Plans have been made to restore some sections of the double track but as yet these have not been implemented.

WESTON-SUPER-MARE ASHCOMBE ROAD
ST 329617

Opened: 1.12.1897 with the opening of the Weston-super-Mare – Clevedon section of the Weston, Clevedon & Portishead Light Railway.

Closed: 20.5.1940 with closure of the line.

Located at the junction of Milton Road and Ashcombe Road, the former office of the 'Traffic Manager of the Railway' survives today with a pharmacy on the ground floor. Alongside the building a metalled path leads east along the former trackbed beside which was a wooden platform and a separate wooden station building with a semi-circular corrugated iron roof. Today there is no trace of either of these structures.

WESTON-SUPER-MARE LOCKING ROAD ST 326612

Opened: c1866 as an additional facility for excursion trains adjacent to the second Weston-super-Mare station. Some rebuilding took place in 1907 but on 8th April 1914 a major development of the old excursion platform into a full station opened.

Closed: 6.9.1964.

By the 1960s most day trippers were coming to the resort by car or coach. Locking Road station closed in 1964 and was demolished in 1967. Ironically the site of the station itself, and a number of other sidings used for the storage of excursion trains, are now covered by roads and car parks associated with the new Tesco supermarket and also further car and coach parking east of Francis Fox Road (named after the architect of the 1884 station).

WEST PENNARD ST 566396

Opened: 3.2.1862 with the opening of the Glastonbury – Cole section of the Somerset Central Railway.

Closed: Passengers: 7.3.1966 with closure of the Evercreech Junction – Highbridge line to passenger traffic; Goods: 10.6.1963.

Following closure of the goods yard in 1963 and the withdrawal of passenger services in 1966, the station site was eventually purchased in 1987 and is now the base for a transport company, R C Withers. The station building has been converted into a house. The station master's house continues in residential use. The goods shed, with a major extension, is used for storage.

WHITCHURCH HALT ST 614673

Opened: 1.1.1925 on the Bristol – Radstock line originally opened on 3.9.1873.

Closed: 2.11.1959 with closure of the Bristol – Radstock – Frome line to passenger traffic.

The pagoda style shelter and platform have gone and the shallow cutting in which the halt stood has been infilled. A gap at the west end of the stone parapet of the A37 over bridge north of the site, now filled by a short wooden fence, marks the former entrance to the halt's access path. Just to the north of the road bridge a new housing development that includes the former railway alignment includes a number of road names relating to the railway era: Halt End, Lines Way and Old Bridge Road.

WICK ST LAWRENCE ST 377653

Opened: 1.12.1897 with the opening of the Weston-super-Mare – Clevedon section of the Weston, Clevedon and Portishead Light Railway.

Closed: 20.5.1940 with closure of the line.

No trace of this halt, at which the small building was a combined booking office and shelter, can now be seen.

WILLITON ST 086416

Opened: 31.3.1862 with the opening of the West Somerset Railway, Norton Junction – Watchet.

Closed: Passengers: 4.1.1971 with closure of the Minehead branch, Norton Junction – Minehead; Goods: 6.7.1964.

Reopened: 28.8.1976 with the opening of the Blue Anchor – Williton section of the restored West Somerset Railway.

Since its reopening by the West Somerset Railway in 1976, the main station building on the down (towards Minehead) platform (now Grade II listed) has been extensively renovated, including the waiting room furniture. South of the building a former store is now a small shop and cafe. The former was originally housed in the restored waiting shelter on the up side which is to be developed as a bookshop. Beyond the new shop/buffet is the 1875 signal box closed in 1971 but now restored to use, being the only Bristol & Exeter Railway era box still in working order. At the south end of the station is a level crossing with hand operated gates mechanically linked with the nearby signal box frame. South of the crossing is a small original stone building now used as a store and a typical corrugated iron lamp room, originating from Taunton.

The two platforms were initially linked by an 1874 covered footbridge north of the station building and up side waiting shelter. This was replaced in the 1920s by an open latticed bridge at the south end of the platform adjacent to the signal box. This in turn was demolished in the late 1960s. Early in the 1990s the GWR era footbridge at Trowbridge (Wilts) was purchased and brought to Williton. Lack of funds prevented its installation. On visiting the site in August 2010 the author was told that it had recently been taken away for restoration, it being planned to erect it at the site of the 1874 footbridge (it was erected on 16 March 2011). In 2001 GWR style lighting was introduced at the station.

The large 1862 goods shed on the down side north of the station building has been the home of the Diesel and Electric Preservation Group since the early 1980s. It was used as a workshop until an adjacent new larger shed was constructed. The goods shed itself was extended at the Minehead end and the DEPG established the building as their Heritage Diesel Visitor Centre; incorporating an education facility it opened officially in 2003. The other current feature at Williton is the prefabricated steel framed vault roofed building at the north end of the goods yard beyond the goods shed. Built in 1899 and now listed Grade II, it stood until 1992 in the GWR Swindon works. It was transferred to its new site in sections and since 1995 has been established as the West Somerset Railway's locomotive headquarters with facilities for the maintenance and overhaul of steam locomotives.

WINCANTON ST 710283

Opened: 3.2.1862 with the opening of the Cole – Templecombe section of the Dorset Central Railway.

Closed: Passengers: 7.3.1966 with closure of the Bath – Poole line to passenger traffic; Goods: 5.4.1965.

Today all traces of the station and goods yard have gone. A number of remnants could be seen until the 1980s but housing now covers the whole site. Leading off Station Road is Pines Close, a reminder of the past era when the Pines Express from Manchester to Bournemouth passed through Wincanton. The foundations of the old signal box remain in the garden of no 42.

WINSCOMBE (SOMERSET) ST 419577

Opened: 3.8.1869 with the opening of the Yatton – Cheddar section of the Cheddar Valley & Yatton Railway. *Opened as Woodborough but renamed Winscombe from 1.12.1869. The suffix 'Somerset' added 12.1.1906.*

Closed: Passengers: 9.9.1963 with closure of the Yatton – Witham line to passenger traffic; Goods: 10.6.1963.

Following closure of the station in 1963, the 1905 GWR style building, which had replaced the original 1869 wooden structure was demolished but the platform and sections of railings and gates were left. The Cheddar Valley Railway Walkway was developed along the former trackbed from Yatton to Axbridge and Cheddar. In 2000 the station site was renovated and developed by Winscombe and Sandford Parish Council as the 'Old Station Millennium Green'. This work included renovation of the platform itself on which the foundations of the former building were exposed. At the northern end is the former bay platform and to the south are restored sections of railway railings and gates. GWR style seats have been placed on the platform. In 2010 the site is a major feature on the now renamed Strawberry Line pedestrian and cycleway, a reminder of the former popular name of the Yatton to Wells railway that reflects the use of the line for both the conveyance of strawberries away from the Cheddar Valley and the annual transport of strawberry pickers to the area.

WITHAM ST 746409

Opened: 1.9.1856 with the opening of the Frome – Yeovil section of the Wilts, Somerset & Weymouth Railway. *Suffix 'Somerset' added 9.6.1958 to distinguish it from the station in Essex.*

Closed: Passengers: 3.10.1966 together with some other stations on the Frome – Yeovil line but three years after the closure of the Yatton to Witham line to passenger traffic on 9.9.1963; Goods: 30.12.1963.

Following closure to passengers in 1966 the station buildings were soon demolished; the wooden branch line platform train shed had been demolished some six years earlier. The station site can still be identified at track side but no significant remnants of the station itself survive. The former railway cottages adjacent to and north of the road bridge continue in residential use, that nearest to the bridge being named 'The Old Station House'.

WIVELISCOMBE   ST 085277

Opened: 8.6.1871 with the opening of the Norton Junction –
Wiveliscombe section of the Devon & Somerset Railway.
Closed: Passengers: 3.10.1966 with closure of the Norton
Junction – Barnstaple line; Goods: 6.7.1964.
On the eastern edge of the town, Station Road leads into an
industrial area in which both the station building and goods
shed survive. The former is an office for a construction firm,
the open waiting area now filled in behind a small surviving
section of the paved up (towards Norton Fitzwarren)
platform. The goods shed, with road side canopy, is still there
in industrial/storage use.

WOOKEY   ST 531463

Opened: 1.8.1871 on the Cheddar – Wells section of the
Cheddar Valley & Yatton Railway originally opened on
8.4.1870.
Closed: Passengers: 9.9.1963 with closure of the Yatton –
Witham line to passenger traffic; Goods: 10.6.1963.
The station building and signal box have gone but the goods
shed survives within an industrial development 'Station Yard'.
When seen in May 2010 the shed was in use by the Wells
Garage body shop. The station master's house continues in
residential use on the east side of Wookey Hole Road, south
of the station site, 'Old Station House'.

WORLE   ST 355618

Opened: 1.3.1884 with the opening of the Weston-super-
Mare loop line.
Closed: 2.1.1922.
Following closure in 1922, the main stone building on the
up (north) side of the line remained for some 40 years until
demolition in the mid 1960s when housing development
took place in the area north of the loop line. Stone from
the demolished building was purchased and used in the
construction of the building erected behind the surviving
Blagdon station.

WORLE PARKWAY   ST 369625

Opened: 24.9.1990 on the Bristol – Bridgwater line originally
opened on 14.6.1841.
Closed: Passengers: remains open principally for trains on
local services on the Bristol – Taunton – Exeter line but is also
served by peak hour trains to and from London (Paddington).
This modern station, built at a cost of some £700,000 was
constructed of lightweight materials because of its site on
marshy ground. A ramped footbridge links the two platforms
on which there are metal and glass shelters, two on the up
platform (towards Bristol) and one on the down. Its original
purpose was as one of the new breed of Parkway stations
providing extensive parking at the station on the outskirts of
towns (one of the first was Bristol Parkway opened in 1972).
In 2010 it is simply called Worle in the timetable but has a
car park for some 130 cars which was virtually full when seen
in late September 2010.

WORLE TOWN   ST 357627

Opened: 1.12.1897 with the opening of the Weston-
super-Mare – Clevedon section of the Weston, Clevedon
& Portishead Light Railway. *Originally Worle Town, Worle
(Moor Lane) from 1913 and then from 1917 Worle Town.*
Closed: 20.5.1940 with closure of the line.
No trace of this station now exists, though originally a
building incorporated a booking office and waiting room. An
original low wooden platform was later removed. Shelter was
also provided by a small wooden hut.

WRINGTON   ST 469625

Opened: 4.12.1901 with the opening of the Wrington Vale
Light Railway, Congresbury – Blagdon.
Closed: Passengers: 14.9.1931 with closure of the line to
passenger traffic; Goods: 10.6.1963 with closure of the
Congresbury – Wrington section of the line to goods traffic.
The whole station site has been redeveloped, including the
Wrington Veterinary Centre and housing, with one of the
roads called Old Station Close. The first house on the Close
is 'The Sidings' with an engine motif on the house number.
The name is a slight exaggeration as Wrington had only one
goods siding in a small yard with a loading dock and crane.
Even less appropriate is a house opposite the station site on
Station Road called 'The Signal Box' as no such facility ever
existed on the Wrington Vale Light Railway!

YATTON   ST 425661

Opened: 14.6.1841 with the opening of the Bristol –
Bridgwater section of the Bristol & Exeter Railway. *Opened
as Clevedon Road, the name changed to Yatton from
28.7.1847 with the opening of the branch line from the
station to Clevedon.*
Closed: Passengers: remains open for trains both for local
services on the Bristol – Weston-super-Mare – Taunton
line and also for peak hour services to and from London
(Paddington); Goods: 29.11.1965.
Decline came in the late 1950s and 1960s, in particular
with the closure of the Cheddar Valley line to Axbridge and
Cheddar and the Clevedon branch. The bay platforms at
the west end of the station, which accommodated these
services, were cleared and the land has been redeveloped for
car parking behind what are now the single face up (towards
Bristol) and down platforms. The canopy towards the west
end of the down platform was also removed as were the
two water tanks that for some years dominated the down
platform. The two original 1841 buildings (both listed) on the
up and down platforms remain as does the canopy on the
west end of the up platform building which was transferred
from the closed Dauntsey (Wilts) station in 1956 replacing
the earlier large canopy that had protected passengers both
on the up main platform and the Clevedon branch platform.

When seen in September 2010 the down side building was
being renovated in readiness for the opening of a community
café serving walkers at the northern end of the 'Strawberry
Line', a pedestrian and cycleway (National Cycle Network
No 26) that has been developed south from Yatton station

on the trackbed of the former line to Axbridge and Cheddar. This Strawberry Line café opened on 13th December 2010. Inside the waiting room beside the booking office on the up platform is a small display of early memorabilia including milk consignment rates and parcel bills dated 1894 and 1895. The footbridge roof has gone and the goods yard, closed in 1965, is now occupied by commercial users, though the goods shed has gone. The station gardens are well tended by local volunteers with support from local firms. 'The Railway Inn', behind the up platform, serves local residents and passengers. The station master's house is in residential use beside the station approach road on the up side, 'Station House'.

YEOVIL HENDFORD   ST 548153

Opened: 1.10.1853 for passenger services as the terminus of the Durston – Yeovil Hendford branch from the Bristol & Exeter Railway.
Closed: Passengers: 1.6.1861 with the opening of Yeovil Town station on the Salisbury – Yeovil section of the Salisbury & Yeovil Railway, originally opened on 6.6.1860; Goods: 9.10.1967.
Today the area where the station and goods depot stood has been redeveloped, accessed principally from Lysander Road. A walkway has been created from the former site of Yeovil Town station to a point on Lysander Road close to its junction with Pine Tree Avenue. Yeovil Hendford station was on the north side of this walkway alongside the south wall of the Allied Carpets store. The Railway Hotel, at the bottom of Hendford Hill (A30) is a reminder of the earlier railway activity in the area.

YEOVIL HENDFORD HALT   ST 546153

Opened: 2.5.1932 on the Durston – Yeovil line originally opened for passenger services on 1.10.1853.
Closed: 15.6.1964 with closure of the Taunton – Yeovil line to passenger traffic.
This 1930s halt was close to the north side of Lysander Road, near today's McDonalds Restaurant. Two old metal gateposts close to the restaurant are relics of railway activity either at the halt or an adjacent siding serving nearby factories. The walkway from Yeovil Town along the former trackbed does not extend across Lysander Road.

YEOVIL JUNCTION   ST 570141

Opened: 19.7.1860 with the opening of the Yeovil Junction – Exeter section of the London & South Western Railway.
Closed: Passengers: remains open for services on the London (Waterloo) – Exeter line.
Today the principal structures erected in a 1907-1909 rebuild remain, though only the former up (north) side island platform continues in railway use for the trains on the London to Exeter line. On this platform are the booking office and the Edwardian style refreshment room 'Pepper's Buffet' which retains several of its original features including the

windows and old counter. Following closure of the former down platform in the mid 1960s the covered footbridge was truncated beyond the north side island. The goods sheds on both the up and down sides remain, the former used by a roofing contractor. The station master's house remains in residential use, 'High Croft'. The South West Main Line Steam Company, founded in 1993, has a 99 year lease on a 1.5 hectare site on the south side of the station. The 1947 turntable has been restored to working order, a water tower (ex Morlands Factory, Glastonbury) erected and a four berth engine shed built. The Company operates the Yeovil Railway Centre, which was officially named in October 1993 at the opening of the engine shed. A recent acquisition was the ex GWR 1864 transfer shed, a listed building at the west end of the site, which now houses an art gallery and visitor centre. This was the venue for special events associated with the Yeovil 150 Celebrations in July 2010.

YEOVIL PEN MILL   ST 570162

Opened: 1.9.1856 with the opening of the Frome – Yeovil section of the Wilts, Somerset & Weymouth Railway.
Closed: Passengers: remains open for services on the Bristol – Yeovil – Weymouth line; Goods: 12.9.1965.
Activity declined at Pen Mill from the 1960s in particular with the closure of the line to Taunton but the station buildings are today largely unaltered. The covered footbridge and platform canopies remain though the small canopy over the station entrance has gone. Cycle stands have recently been installed on the forecourt. In 1934 the current canopies replaced an overall timber roof, similar to that surviving today at Frome. The booking office area was revamped and opened by the local MP, Paddy Ashdown, on 3rd December 1993. A buffet, 'Puffing Billy' operates in the former parcels office on the up single face platform. The signal box at the north end of the station continues in use, operating the semaphore signals in the station area.

YEOVIL TOWN   ST 562158

Opened: 1.6.1861 on the Sherborne – Yeovil Hendford section of the Salisbury – Yeovil Railway originally opened on 1.6.1860.
Closed: Passengers: 2.10.1966 with the withdrawal of a shuttle service from Yeovil Junction; Goods: 3.5.1965.
Today there is virtually no trace of this station opened 150 years ago in June 1861. The sole remnant is the foundation stone with the date 1860, re-erected in a paved area within a large retail/leisure complex developed in recent years over the entire station site. Prior to this the site was used for some 30 years as a car park after the station buildings were demolished in the early 1970s. To the north of the new development the long road bridge that carried Newton Road over the lines remains in place; under its arches is the access to a large car park and also a walkway created along the former trackbed to Yeovil Pen Mill station.

FURTHER READING

Atthill R., *The Somerset and Dorset Railway*, David and Charles, 1967

Butt R.V.J., *Directory of Railway Stations*, Patrick Stephens, 1995

Castens S., *On the Trail of the Titfield Thunderbolt*, Thunderbolt Books, 2000

Clark R.H., *An Historical Survey of Selected Great Western Railway Stations, Layouts and Illustrations*, Oxford Publishing Co., Volume 1, 1976, Volume 2, 1979, Volume 3, 1981

Clinker C.R., *Register of Closed Passenger Stations and Goods Depots 1830-1977*, Avon Anglia, 1978

Cubitt E. and Stanistreet A., *Stations and Buildings of the West Somerset Railway*, West Somerset Railway Association, 5th Edition, 2007

Dale P., *Somerset's Lost Railways*, Stenlake Publishing, 2001

Deacon T., *The Somerset & Dorset: Aftermath of the Beeching Axe*, Oxford Publishing Co., 1995

Dowling G. and Whitehouse J., *British Railways Past and Present No 16, Avon, Cotswolds and the Malverns*, Silver Link Publishing, 1993

Fry P., *Railways into Wells*, Somerset and Dorset Railway Trust, 1998

Gosling T. and Clement M., *Somerset Railways*, Sutton Publishing, 2000

Gough T., *The Southern – West of Salisbury*, Oxford Publishing Co., 1984

Hammond A., *S & D Memories*, Millstream Books, 1993

Harrison J.D., *The Bridgwater Railway*, Oakwood Press, 1990

Hawkins M., *Somerset & Dorset, Then and Now*, David and Charles, 1995

Hawkins M, *LSWR West Country Lines Then and Now*, David and Charles, 1993

Hayes R. and Shaw M., *Railways in Wells*, HST, 1982/1986

Judge C.W. and Potts C.R., *Somerset and Dorset Railway: An Historical Survey of Track Layouts and Illustrations*, Oxford Publishing Co., 1979

Leigh C., *GWR Country Stations*, Ian Allan, Volume 1 1981/1985, Volume 2 1984

Leitch R., *The Railways of Keynsham*, RCTS, 1997

Lund B. and Laming P., *Somerset Railway Stations on Old Picture Postcards*. Reflections of a By-gone Age, 2005

Madge R., *Railways around Exmoor*, The Exmoor Press, 1971/1975
Somerset Railways, The Dovecote Press, 1984

Maggs C.G., *Branch Lines of Somerset*, Alan Sutton, 1993
Bristol Railway Panorama, Millstream Books, 1990

GWR Bristol to Bath Line, Sutton Publishing, 2001
GWR Swindon to Bath Line, Sutton Publishing, 2003
Highbridge in its Heyday, Oakwood Press, 1986
Mangotsfield to Bath Branch, Oakwood Press, 1992
Somerset Railways, Somerset Books, 2007
Taunton Steam, Millstream Books, 1991
The Clevedon Branch, Wild Swan Publications, 1987
The Last Years of the Somerset & Dorset, Ian Allan, 1991
Weston, Clevedon & Portishead Railway, Oakwood Press, 1964

Maggs C. G. and Beale G., *The Camerton Branch*, Wild Swan Publications, 1985

Mitchell D., *British Railways Past and Present No 30 Somerset*, Past and Present Publishing Ltd, 1996

Mitchell V. and Smith K., Middleton Press (various publication dates)
Bath Green Park to Bristol, 1999
Bath to Evercreech Junction, 1988
Bournemouth to Evercreech Junction, 1987
Branch Line to Cheddar, 1997
Branch Lines around Chard and Yeovil, 1999
Branch Lines to Clevedon and Portishead, 2003
Branch Line to Minehead, 1990
Bristol to Taunton, 2003
Burnham to Evercreech Junction, 1989
Frome to Bristol, 1986
Salisbury to Yeovil, 1992
Swindon to Bristol, 2002
Taunton to Barnstaple, 1995
Taunton to Exeter, 2002
Westbury to Bath, 1995
Westbury to Taunton, 2002
Yeovil to Dorchester, 1990
Yeovil to Exeter, 1991

Peters I., *The Somerset & Dorset*, Oxford Publishing Co., 1974

Phillips D., *Steaming through the Cheddar Valley,* Ian Allan, 2002
Westbury to Weymouth Line, Oxford Publishing Co., 1994
Working Yeovil to Taunton Steam, Fox and Co., 1991

Phillips D. and Pryer G., *Salisbury to Exeter Line*, Oxford Publishing Co., 1997

Phillips D. and Eaton-Lacey R., *Working the Chard Branch*, Fox and Co., 1991

Potts C., *An Historical Survey of Selected Great Western Railway Stations, Layouts and Illustrations*, Oxford

Publishing Co., Volume 4, 1985

Pryer G. and Bowring G., *An Historical Survey of Selected Southern Stations, Track Layouts and Illustrations,* Oxford Publishing Company, Volume 1, 1980

Quick M. E., *Railway Passenger Stations in England, Scotland and Wales,* RCMS 2nd Edition 2003, Supplement, 2005

Robertson K., *Great Western Railway Halts,* Volume 1, Irwell Press, 1990, Volume 2, KRB Publications, 2002
Somerset and Avon Railways in Old Photographs, Alan Sutton, 1990

Sellick R., *The Old Mineral Line,* The Exmoor Press, 1981

Smith M., *The Railways of Bristol & Somerset,* Ian Allan, 1992

Strange P., *Weston, Clevedon & Portishead Railway,* Twelveheads Press, 1989

Stretton J., *The West Somerset Railway, A Past and Present Companion,* Past and Present Publishing Ltd, 2000

Thomas D.St.J. *Regional History of the Railways of Great Britain,* Volume 1, The West Country, David and Charles, 1981

Vaughan A., *Great Western Architecture: A Pictorial Record,* Oxford Publishing Co., 1977
GWR Junction Stations, Ian Allan, 1988

Vincent M. *Reflections on the Portishead Branch,* Oxford Publishing Co. 1983
Through Countryside & Coalfield, Oxford Publishing Co., 1990

Waters L., *Great Western Railway – Then and Now,* Ian Allan, Volume 1 1994, Volume 2, 2002

Williams D.J., *The West Somerset Railway, A Past and Present Companion,* Volume 2, Past and Present Publishing Ltd, 2009

ACKNOWLEDGEMENTS

The author is very grateful for permission to use photographs from the following collections:

Colin Caddy; Pages 7,13 (top), 15 (middle), 19 (top), 19 (middle lower), 22 (middle lower), 23 (top), 25 (top), 26 (middle), 36 (top), 36 (middle lower), 37 (middle lower), 38 (top), 40 (top), 43 (top), 43 (middle lower), 44 (top), 47 (top), 53 (middle lower), 57 (top), 58 (middle), 73 (top), 74 (top), 75 (top), 78 (top), 81 (top), 82 (middle lower), 83 (top) 84 (top), 86 (bottom left), 87 (bottom left), 89 (top), 90 (middle lower), 96 (top), 99 (top), 102 (top), 107 (top), 110 (top), 110 (bottom left), 112 (top).

Lens of Sutton; Pages 20 (top), 21 (top), 21 (middle lower), 27 (top), 33 (middle lower), 34 (top), 35 (top), 41 (middle), 46 (top), 48 (top), 49 (top), 51 (top), 52 (top), 52 (bottom left), 54 (top), 66 (middle lower), 68 (top), 71 (bottom left), 76 (top), 76 (middle), 79 (middle), 80 (top), 80 (middle), 86 (top), 98 (top), 102 (bottom left), 108 (top), 108 (bottom left), 109 (top), 111 (top).

Mike Tozer; Pages 17 (top), 42 (top), 50 (top), 62 (top), 64 (top), 66 (top), 67 (top), 68 (bottom left), 70 (top), 87 (top), 90 (top), 92 (bottom left), 93 (top), 104 (top).

Roger Carpenter; Pages 14 (top), 14 (bottom left), 26 (top), 29 (top), 31 (bottom right), 33 (top), 53 (top), 109 (middle).

R.K.Blencowe; Pages 30 (middle), 32 (middle lower), 37 (top), 42 (middle), 58 (bottom), 61 (top), 65 (top), 71 (top), 103 (top), 111 (middle).

Colin Maggs; Pages 18 (top), 58 (top), 60 (middle), 95 (top), 106 (top).

The remaining photographs were taken by the author or are from his collection where the copyright is unknown or unclear.